HOW TO BE CLEVER

by

Ben Pridmore

Contents

How To Be Clever……………………………………………………………....…..3

How To Memorise A Pack Of Cards……………………………………...….....5

How To Name The Day Of The Week For Any Given Date………...11

How To Multiply Long Numbers In Your Head………………………18

How To Memorise Numbers…………………………………………………23

How To Win At Blackjack……………………………………………………....30

How To Get Into Mensa…………………………………………………….......40

How To Not Play Chess……………………………………………………….50

How To Calculate Square Roots……………………………………....……63

How To Be Creative…………………………………………………………......69

How To Win The World Memory Championship……………….....72

ISBN 978-1-257-09904-7
Published by lulu.com

(No real publishers wanted it)

How To Be Clever

So, what's this book all about?

It does what it says on the tin. This book will teach you how to be clever. But it's important to note that when I say 'clever', I don't mean the same as 'intelligent'.

What's the difference?

Intelligence is something you're born with. Some people have a lot of it, and some people very little. But there are a lot of people out there with only an average amount of intelligence, but who are regarded by everyone who knows them as 'a really clever person'. Cleverness, as I see it, is a mixture of four things – intelligence, knowledge, memory and creativity.

Intelligence I can't do anything about. But the aim of this book is to teach you a few lessons in the knowledge that can amaze everyone you speak to, the memory to help you recall it, and the creativity to use it in the right place.

Put it all together, and people will THINK you're clever. Even if you're not.

What's the benefit of being thought of as clever if I'm not?

There are many, many benefits! The main one is that if people think you're clever, they'll think you're right when you express an opinion. They'll assume you know what you're talking about on any subject, even if you've never shown any knowledge about it before. They'll even assume you're good at your job, however totally incompetent you might be. Believe me, it's a great thing to have a reputation as a clever person.

What's with all the footnotes?

Well noticed. On every page of this book, you'll find an asterisk pointing you to a footnote at the bottom of the page.* Sometimes these footnotes

---

* Like this.

will be something to do with the main subject matter of the page. More often, they won't be. The footnotes constitute interesting pieces of knowledge that you will hopefully remember and be able to drop into conversation at appropriate times. A good knowledge of interesting trivia is the number one way to make people think you're clever!

And I'd just like to make it clear that all the trivia items you'll find in the footnotes of this book are TRUE. They're not the kind of thing you'll see on the internet or in bulk emails forwarded around the office.[*] Everything in this book has been scrupulously checked and double-checked, and not on Wikipedia, either. You can quote these facts with confidence, they have my personal guarantee.

Who are you?

I'm Ben Pridmore. I have at various times been World Memory Champion, World Intelligence Champion and World Decamentathlon Champion, won gold medals at the Mind Sports Olympiad in five different events, and represented Britain at the Mental Calculation World Cup and the World Othello Championship. I'm a member of Mensa and regularly quoted as a well-known clever person.

This list of achievements testifies more than anything to the huge number of ways anyone can make people believe they're clever. There are no end of competitions out there with impressive-sounding titles that practically nobody has ever heard of, and getting a high placing in one of them takes very little effort, just because there are very few competitors. Using the tricks in this book, you too can achieve a meaningless accolade to put after your name for the rest of time!

I was also on The Weakest Link once. I came fourth.

Who am I?

You're the reader's voice. Throughout this book, you will be asking both clever and stupid questions, which I will then answer in entirely clever and not at all stupid ways.

Where do we start?

---

[*] Well, most or all of the footnotes in this book probably can be found on the internet. Everything can be found on the internet nowadays. But the point is that the internet also contains a lot of 'facts' that are completely wrong, and this book doesn't.

Just turn the page. And one more word of advice – don't take this book too seriously. Have fun with it!

How To Memorise A Pack Of Cards

This doesn't sound like something I could do.

Actually, it's much, much easier to do than you might think. In fact, I would go so far as to say that anyone can do it with just a tiny bit of practice, and knowing the trick that makes it all a lot easier. Before I get to that, here's some trivia that you shouldn't let put you off learning this skill: the current world-record time for memorising a pack of cards is 26.28 seconds. Ten years ago it was considered impossible to do it in less than three minutes, but you too can do the impossible, I guarantee it, by following these simple instructions.

Did you invent this method?

No, the basic principle dates from long before my time. It was probably invented by an ancient Greek called Simonides, who having invented it then didn't do anything with it and left it to be reinvented centuries later by people who wanted to be clever. It's called the location method, and it involves using mental pictures of people or objects in set locations. Some people also call it the journey method, because it involves these locations being in a set sequence, and most people like their mental locations to be points on a journey. Lots of people over the years have added their own twists to the basic principles, and the specific system described below is my version. If you don't like it, you might prefer to buy the books by Tony Buzan, Dominic O'Brien and Andi Bell (although none of them has useless knowledge at the bottom of every page like this one)[*]

To memorise a pack of cards, then, you first need to think of a journey or route with 26 easily-remembered locations. All the routes I use are either around different rooms of large buildings (my old school provides three routes – the first one starts in room 6, then moves onto room 5, room 4, the hallway, the top of the stairs, the bottom of the stairs, the downstairs hallway, room 3, room 2, room 1 and so on. Your old school was probably laid out in a different kind of way, but you get the idea), or around a town (corner shop, roundabout, t-junction, newsagents etc). As

---

[*] For example, The national anthem of Vanuatu is called "Yumi, Yumi, Yumi". It means "We, We, We", and goes on to add "… are happy to proclaim that we, we, we are the people of Vanuatu!"

long as it's a familiar kind of journey and you can mentally picture the 26 points in the right order, it doesn't matter where you go. Write it down, so you've got it handy to come back to after the second bit of preparation. Here's another of mine as an example, with space to write yours beside it (see, I think of everything!). If you know your way around Skegness, you might be able to follow mine around the town.[*]

1. train station platform   1.
2. train station café   2.
3. outside the station   3.
4. pedestrian crossing   4.
5. taxi rank   5.
6. charity shop on the corner   6.
7. bank halfway down the road   7.
8. sweet shop a bit further down   8.
9. clock tower   9.
10. chip shop around the corner   10.
11. gift shop outside the park   11.
12. amusement arcade further down the road   12.
13. pedestrian crossing   13.
14. bingo hall in the pier amusements   14.
15. the next room of the pier amusements   15.
16. and the next   16.
17. and the next   17.
18. outside on the pier   18.
19. down at the bottom of the steps   19.
20. bridge over the river   20.
21. outside another amusement arcade   21.
22. inside the arcade   22.
23. out the other side, by the big dipper   23.
24. the other end of the funfair   24.
25. out of the funfair, by the river   25.
26. the car park over the road   26.

Have you spent a lot of time playing video games in Skegness?

Yep. It's not essential for developing memory skills, though. Pick anywhere you've spent a lot of time walking around.

---

[*] The national anthem of Vanuatu is in the Bislama language. This is a wonderful language, because it has two different words for 'we', depending whether the word is inclusive or exclusive of the person addressed. 'We' in the sense of 'you and me' is 'yumi', whereas 'we' in the sense of 'me and this other fellow' is 'mifala'.

The second bit is the images of objects or people we mentioned earlier. We're going to create 52 of these, and associate each of them with a different playing card, so that every time you see the ace of hearts, you'll think of a hat, and visualise it at the appropriate point of your route.

Why can't I just visualise the ace of hearts on my route instead?

Well, you can try, but take it from me that it doesn't work. Playing cards all look too similar, and they can get mixed up in your brain very easily. The seven of clubs is a lot like the eight of clubs, but a key isn't anything like a cone.

But it's all very well to say 'The ace of hearts is a hat', but how do you remember that? There's a method for converting cards (and, in the next chapter, numbers) into images in a way that will jog your memory every time you use it.

The first thing to look at is the suit of the cards. All the hearts will be turned into a word that starts with H, all the clubs into a word that starts with C, and so on. We'll start with the suit of hearts. Each card will be represented by a word starting with a 'h' sound. The next sound in the word is determined by the number of the card, as follows.

Choose your own words – each one should be the first that comes into your mind when you think "What starts with 'ha'?" That way, whenever you see the ace of hearts, you'll think of that word, and the picture that goes with it.[*]

Ace = 'a' – hat, hand, ham, hankie, Harry
2 = 'e' – hen, hem, heron, hell, head
3 = 'i' – hippo, hill, history
4 = 'o' – holly, hockey stick, hog
5 = 'u' – hut, hook, hummingbird, hubcap
6 = 'A' – hay, haze, hake, hail
7 = 'E' – heater, he-man, heel
8 = 'I' – hi-fi, high-chair, hide
9 = 'O' – hoe, hose, hotel
10 = 'U' or 'oo' – hoop, hula, hooter, Hugh
Jack = 'ow' – house, hound, howler
Queen = 'or' – horse, horn, hawk

---

[*] "Yummy Yummy Yummy", on the other hand, was a hit for Ohio Express, reaching number 5 in the British charts in the summer of 1968.

King = 'ar' – heart, harp, harness

It's important to note that it's the sound of the word we're interested in, not the spelling. Our brains process sounds a lot quicker than they process written words. So 'hook' can be the five of hearts, but shouldn't be the four. Of course, if you don't speak with the same accent as me, it might be the ten... When you've picked a word for each card, make sure you can visualise a picture of that object or person. Know what kind of hat you're thinking of, what colour, what shape, what size. And once you're happy with the hearts, here are some suggestions for the other three suits[*]:

	Clubs	Spades	Diamonds
Ace	cat, can, camel, carrot	sand, Sam, sack, sash	Dan, dam, dagger, dad
2	kettle, Ken, kestrel, Kelly	sellotape, settee, setter	Den, deckchair, Del
3	kitten, kiss, kipper	scissors, signature, signet, sieve	digger, dinner, dipper
4	cot, comic, collar, cog	sausage, salt, sock	dot, doll, dog, dock
5	custard, cutter, cook	soot, sun, sucker, sub	dummy, duck
6	case, Katy, cane, cake	safe, sail, sabre, sailor	daisy, date, Dale
7	key, keel, keeper	sea, seal, seed, seat	Dean, DJ, demon
8	kite, Kylie	cyclops, silo, sine wave	dice, dial, diver
9	coat, cone, coal, cobra	soap, sofa, sole	dough, donut, dome
10	cue, cooler, cube	suit, sumo, soup	dew, dune
Jack	cow, cowl, cowboy	sow, sound	dowel, down

---

[*] A first cousin is someone with whom you share a grandparent – one of your parents is the brother or sister of one of your first cousin's parents. A second cousin is someone with whom you share a great-grandparent – one of your grandparents is the brother or sister of one of your second cousin's grandparents. A cousin once removed is the son or daughter of your cousin. A cousin twice removed is your cousin's grandchild. Or grandparent.

| Queen | core, corn, cork | saw, sauce, sorter | door, doorman, Dawn |
| King | car, cart, calf, card | sari, sergeant, sarnie, Sara | dart, dalek, dark |

Make sure that all your 52 images are different enough from each other that you won't get them confused. Then see if you can remember the whole list without looking at it. If you get stuck, you can just think 'what starts with ca?', and the word should come back to you. Get a pack of cards and pick one at random a few times, and see how quickly you can visualise the appropriate image.

And now we put the images and the journey together?

Right! Take a pack of cards and shuffle it well (they're easier to memorise if they're not shuffled, but people aren't nearly as impressed that way).

Turn over the first two cards. We're going to put two images at each point on the route. For example, the first two cards in the pack I've got in front of me are the eight of diamonds and the three of clubs. So, depending on your list and your journey, you might imagine something like a dice rolling towards a kitten on the platform of Skegness railway station. Make sure you can tell what order the two images come in – have the first card-image be on the left, or on top of the second one. And be consistent with this throughout the 26 pairs of images. It's good to have the images interact or come into contact with each other, because it makes the whole tableau more memorable.

Moving onto the next stop on my journey, which is a café on Skegness train station which closed down years ago but used to have a Donkey Kong machine in the corner long after everywhere else in Skegness had moved on to more modern video games, I've got a digger (three of diamonds) unearthing a safe (six of spades) in the middle of the café. If the cards had been the other way around, I would have had the safe contain a miniature digger. After a bit of practice, the images develop rules about how they relate to each other in either sequence, and it becomes impossible to get them the wrong way round.[*]

---

[*] Probably the most famous quote from any cricket commentary in history was "The batsman's Holding, the bowler's Willey." Yes, there's nothing wrong with a little childish humour, even if you're trying to make people think you're clever. What really is clever, though, is being able to mention the first names of Holding and Willey if it comes up in conversation – they were Michael and Peter. And

Go on through the pack until you've imagined 26 pairs of images at 26 points on your journey. Look through the pack again another time or two and see how many you can remember, then see if you can say every card before you turn it over and look at it. Easy, isn't it?

So how do I get really fast at it?

Practice! And lots of it. The more packs of cards you memorise, the easier it gets. But don't get so engrossed that you forget to read the rest of this book…[*]

---

incidentally, Holding was the batsman. Make sure to correct anyone who says it the other way around.

[*] Especially not the footnotes.

How To Name The Day Of The Week For Any Given Date

Is that even possible?

Yes, it is. You don't have to be a natural genius to do it, either (although it helps). It takes a combination of memory skills and mental arithmetic, and with a bit of practice, you can put a day to any date, past, present or future, in a matter of seconds.

Will it make people think I'm clever?

Definitely. Ask someone to tell you their birthdate, tell them what day it was, and they'll be hugely impressed. It works particularly well as a chat-up line if the person you're talking to was born on a Monday, as you can add something along the lines of "But of course I could tell that as soon as I saw you, as Monday's child is fair of face, and all that."[*]

Great! So, how do you do it?

You need to work out four numbers, and add them together. The numbers come from the day, month, year and century of the date given:

Day – This is the easiest to work out. Simply subtract seven from the number until you're left with something between 0 and 6. So, for the 13th of a month, the number is 6. For the 29th, the number is 1. For the 14th, the number is 0.

Month – There is a different number for each month, as follows:

---

[*] Note: this might not work. Also, be warned that some people take violent exception to being told that they are bonny and blithe and good and gay. What, you don't know the rhyme?

"Monday's child is fair of face,
Tuesday's child is full of grace,
Wednesday's child is full of woe,
Thursday's child has far to go,
Friday's child is loving and giving,
Saturday's child works hard for a living,
But the child that is born on the Sabbath day
Is bonny and blithe and good and gay."

If you're using this technique as a chat-up line, it might be best to pretend that the person you're talking to was born on a Monday or Friday.

- January = 1
- February = 4
- March = 4
- April = 0
- May = 2
- June = 5
- July = 0
- August = 3
- September = 6
- October = 1
- November = 4
- December = 6

The best way to remember this is to memorise the 12-digit number 144025036146. If you're using the advanced number-memory system outlined in the last chapter of this book, that can become a mental image of four three-figure numbers. For me, it's TORo [a 1940s superhero whom few people nowadays will have heard of], SELlotaping his SIGnature to a TOGgle. If, on the other hand, you haven't read that chapter, or if you have read it but think it's a stupid system that doesn't work, twelve digits is short enough to memorise by repeating it to yourself over and over. Try it and see.*

Year – There's a number for each year, too, but this time they follow a pattern. It's a complicated pattern, but once you've got the hang of it, you can work it out without needing to memorise 100 different numbers. It goes as follows:

Year	'00	'01	'02	'03	'04	'05	'06	'07	'08	'09	'10	'11	'12	'13	'14	'15	'16	'17	'18	'19
Number	0	1	2	3	5	6	0	1	3	4	5	6	1	2	3	4	6	0	1	2
Year	'20	'21	'22	'23	'24	'25	'26	'27	'28	'29	'30	'31	'32	'33	'34	'35	'36	'37	'38	'39
Number	4	5	6	0	2	3	4	5	0	1	2	3	5	6	0	1	3	4	5	6
Year	'40	'41	'42	'43	'44	'45	'46	'47	'48	'49	'50	'51	'52	'53	'54	'55	'56	'57	'58	'59
Number	1	2	3	4	6	0	1	2	4	5	6	0	2	3	4	5	0	1	2	3
Year	'60	'61	'62	'63	'64	'65	'66	'67	'68	'69	'70	'71	'72	'73	'74	'75	'76	'77	'78	'79
Number	5	6	0	1	3	4	5	6	1	2	3	4	6	0	1	2	4	5	6	0
Year	'80	'81	'82	'83	'84	'85	'86	'87	'88	'89	'90	'91	'92	'93	'94	'95	'96	'97	'98	'99
Number	2	3	4	5	0	1	2	3	5	6	0	1	3	4	5	6	1	2	3	4

---

* Who shot JR? It's a question that has gone down in history (if you missed that history lesson, it's a reference to the American soap opera Dallas), but surprisingly few people know the answer. It was Sue Ellen's evil sister, Kristin.

See the pattern? It restarts every 28 years. Every year it increases by one, except leap years, in which it increases by two. So you can remember it by just remembering the leap years, and counting up from the nearest one. And the leap years have a pattern to them too, going 053164205316420531642 (decreasing by two or increasing by five, whichever way you want to look at it, but going back to 0 when it reaches 7)

So, if you know your 28-times-table, you can remember easily that the years '00, '28, '56 and '84 of any century have a year number of 0. '04, '32, '60, and '88 have a year number of 5, and so on.

This is complicated, I know, but practice it a few times and you'll soon get the hang of it. For example, the year '37. The nearest multiple of 28 is '28. You know that's 0, and from that you can work out that '32 is 5, and '36 is 3. From leap years, if you remember, it goes up in ones, so for the year '37, the year number is 4.

For the year '79, the nearest starting point is '56, going up through the leap years brings us to '76, which is 4 (or you can go the other way and work backwards from '84, of course), add three to get 7, which means 0 (because it's always a number between 0 and 6, so take away 7 whenever you get above that).

Century – This is a much simpler pattern. It would have been even easier if not for Pope Gregory XIII, but we'll get to him in a minute[*]. Until the 18th century, the century codes work like this:

1700s - 1
1600s - 2
1500s - 3
1400s - 4
1300s - 5
1200s - 6
1100s - 0
1000s - 1
900s - 2
800s - 3
700s - 4

---

[*] See the rest of the footnotes in this chapter for details. Another thing Pope Gregory XIII did is make the rules for how they work out the date of Easter each year. It takes place on the first Sunday after the first ecclesiastical full moon after the vernal equinox.

600s - 5
500s - 6
400s - 0
300s - 1

… and so on. Granted, if you're only using this technique as a chat-up line, you're not likely to be talking to anyone who was born this long ago, but sooner or later some smart alec is going to ask you a date like July 23rd, 1492 (it was a Monday, if you're curious. We're nearly finished with the explanations, so stick with me for just a few more paragraphs, and one little essay about the Gregorian calendar, and you'll be able to work it out for yourself!) The best way to remember these is just to get one of them fixed in your mind, 1700s = 1, say, and work back from there, adding one at a time as you go back through the centuries.

But from September 14th, 1752 onwards, the century codes go like this:

1700s - 4
1800s - 2
1900s - 0
2000s - 6
2100s - 4
2200s - 2
2300s - 0
2400s - 6
2500s - 4

…and so on. At the time of writing, it's 2010, and therefore the people you're chatting up are likely to have been born in the 1900s, unless they're schoolchildren or centenarians, so the century number for that is 0.[*]

---

[*] What's an ecclesiastical full moon? Well, Gregory had his astronomers draw up a book of tables enabling them to work out when there would be a full moon for any year in the rest of time. These tables were created with the best of 16th-century knowledge, and so aren't a hundred percent accurate. But they are still used today to calculate the date of Easter, even if the ecclesiastical full moon is a couple of days away from the actual full moon.

What's a vernal equinox? It's the day in the spring when the time from sunrise to sunset is exactly twelve hours, again according to Pope Gregory's calculations.

Why is Easter based on full moons and equinoxes when it commemorates Christ's resurrection? Because the early Christians took over an old pagan spring-festival and made it their own.

What happened on September 14^(th) 1752?

It's a long story, and one that you really don't need to know in order to do this trick. The rest of the footnotes for this chapter go into more detail than anyone could ever need*. If you already know about the Gregorian and Julian Calendars, or if you don't know and don't care, feel free to skip it†:

I skipped it. So, could we get back to the naming-the-day trick now? I've got four numbers and I don't know what to do with them.

Add them together. Subtract seven from the result until you've got a final number between 0 and 6, and you've got the day, as follows:

1. Sunday
2. Monday
3. Tuesday
4. Wednesday
5. Thursday
6. Friday
0. Saturday

---

* Most people know that a year is 365 days long. Most clever people will tell you that it's actually 365¼, which is why we have a leap year every four years, to even it out. Julius Caesar took the credit for introducing this system (although he just stole the idea from the Alexandrians who'd been using it for years, after he conquered Egypt) to the Roman Empire, and thus most of the world of the 1^(st) century BC. With typical modesty, the new calendar became known as the Julian Calendar (and for good measure, one of the months became 'July', just in case anyone forgot who the boss was).

† However, a year isn't exactly 365¼ days long. It's actually about ten minutes less than 365¼, which may not sound like anything worth worrying about, but meant that with an extra day every four years, the calendar was very gradually moving out of synch with the seasons. If left unchecked for tens of thousands of years, January would end up in the middle of summer. In the 16^(th) century, Pope Gregory XIII and the Roman Catholic church realised that this gradual creeping forwards of the calendar meant that Easter wasn't happening at the right time. Accordingly, Gregory issued a decree that all years that are a multiple of 100 but not of 400 would no longer be leap years. So 1600 would have 366 days, but 1700, 1800 and 1900 would only have 365, and so on. He also decided that, to make up for the extra days there had been since Roman times, ten days would be cut out of the calendar. So October 4^(th), 1582 was followed directly by October 15^(th).

(My birthday is actually October 14^(th), so I would have been really annoyed about this if I'd been alive at the time.)

So, let's try a couple of examples. The one above, 23rd July 1492, works out as follows:

23rd = 2 [subtract the closest multiple of 7, which is 21]

July = 0 [the seventh month of the year, so the S of SIGnature, or the seventh digit of 144025036146]

1400s = 4 [1700s = 1, 1600s = 2, 1500s = 3, 1400s = 4]

'92 = 3 ['84 = 0, '88 = 5, '92 = 3]

Adding them together is pretty easy, it comes to 9, which when you take off 7 gives you 2, which is the second day of the week, Monday!*

Hint – The year number is the most complicated calculation you have to do. Because you have to juggle four numbers in your head, it's best to do the hardest calculation first, otherwise you might forget the numbers you've already worked out. Start with the year, then the century, then the month, then the day. Practice makes perfect!

One final rule – If the date is in January or February of a leap year, subtract one from the final total. That extra February 29th messes the whole system up otherwise.

If you didn't read the bit about the Gregorian calendar (you should, you know. It's fascinating.), be aware that every year divisible by 4 is a leap year, but for the year '00, only when the first two digits are divisible by 4

---

* This new calendar was called the Gregorian Calendar, and is the one in use today. But it wasn't used worldwide straight away. All the Catholic countries followed the Pope's instructions and cut ten days out of the year, but in Britain and its colonies, where the official policy was to refuse to do anything the Pope said, the Julian Calendar was defiantly still used for another 170 years.

This, as you can imagine, led to no end of confusion. When it was January 1st in England, it was January 11th in Spain. The British hatred of conforming to European standards, even when they make sense, stopped the new calendar being adopted until they finally gave in in 1752, and switched to the Gregorian Calendar in September. By then there had been another extra day, since 1700 had been a leap year in Britain but not in the Catholic countries, so eleven days were skipped, and September 2nd was followed the next day by September 14th.

as well. So 2000 was a leap year, but 1800 and 1900 weren't, and 2100 won't be either.

So, let's try one more example. I was born on 14th October, 1976.

$14^{th} = 0$

October = 1

1900s = 0

'76 = 4

0 + 1 + 0 + 4 = 5

5 = Thursday. Thursday's child has far to go. Which is perfectly true. I'm only two chapters into writing this book. Ah well, stick with me, and you'll learn a lot more before we get to the back cover. So, what shall we do next?

Actually, I'm going to go out and see if I can chat up someone who was born on a Monday. See you later.

Okay, see you later. Don't forget to awe this fair-faced person with your knowledge of the history of the Gregorian calendar!*

Ah well, I'll just have to wait for the reader to get back. It gets dark here when you close the book, you know…

---

* While we're on the subject of trivia, Britain wasn't the last country to change to the new system – Turkey officially adopted the Gregorian Calendar in 1927.

How To Multiply Long Numbers In Your Head

Can that really be done?

Of course! The trick is to do it a bit at a time and multiply small numbers together, then add them up.

Okay, but isn't it easier to use a calculator?

Well, yes, but it's a lot less impressive. Besides, try using a calculator to multiply 27562946 by 72519463. Unless you've got an unusually big display, the answer's too many digits.

Okay, so I'll use a computer.

Oh, you're no fun. Anyway, for those of you who want to learn this anyway, let's start with something a bit easier. We'll do 396 x 184, which if you're that way inclined you can check on your calculator and find the answer to be 72,864[*].

But before we begin, a quick word on what I mean by 'in your head'. It's not as simple a definition as you might think. The obvious, but more difficult, way to interpret it is that you're not allowed to write anything down and just have to say the answer after juggling the numbers mentally. Official mental calculation competitions and world records allow competitors to write down the answer one digit at a time, starting with the last if they wish, as long as they don't write any intermediate calculations. This makes the whole thing a bit easier, especially with the following method – otherwise, you need to remember the digits you've already worked out while you're working out the rest.

---

[*] As everyone knows, you can't draw a box with a cross in it, like this: without lifting your pen from the paper or going over a line twice. You're always going to have one of the lines missing. Like this:

Try drawing two boxes joined together, like this: and you'll find that you can't do it without two missing lines.

But try drawing a two-by-two stack of boxes with crosses: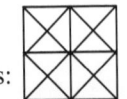

and you can do it with only three lines missing! There's actually a mathematical formula – for any arrangement of boxes like that, x boxes high and y boxes wide, the minimum number of lines you have to leave blank (unless you cheat) is $x + y - 1$.

There are mental calculation competitions?

Yes indeed – there's a Mental Calculation World Championship, held in Britain every year, and a Mental Calculation World Cup, held every two years in Germany. There are probably others, too, and they probably also involve the word 'World' in the title.

So how do you do it?

Take the multiplication one digit at a time, starting from the end. For the sum 396 x 184, we know the final digit of the answer will be the final digit of 6 x 4 – which, if you know your times tables you'll know to be 24. So our last digit is 4 – write it down or remember it, depending on how hard you want to make things for yourself, and carry the 2 into the next calculation.*

Now for the second-last digit. It's less obvious, but this one is made up of the tens from the previous calculation (that 2 we just carried), plus 6 x 8, plus 9 x 4. That is, we're multiplying the last digit of each number with the second-to-last digit of the other number. 2 + 48 + 36 = 86. Once again, we take the last digit of the answer, write it down in front of the 4 we already got, and carry the 8.

Or, to look at it another way, we're taking the first number (396) and gradually multiplying each digit by each digit of the second number (184), working backwards. Carrying on in the same way, our third-from-last digit will be 8 + (6 x 1) + (9 x 8) + (3 x 4), which all adds up to 98.

I'll take your word for it. You expect me to do that in my head?

Try it. It's really not as difficult as you might think, once you've had a little bit of practice and assuming that you know your times tables. As long as you can remember what the product of any two numbers is, you're just adding together a few two-digit numbers. And that really is something that gets easier the more you do it.

---

* Speaking of calculations, everyone knows Pythagoras's Theorem – in a right-angled triangle, the square of the hypotenuse is equal to the sum of the squares on the other two sides – but it's less well known that Pythagoras (an ancient Greek mathematician and philosopher) wasn't the first person to discover it. The ancient Babylonians knew the theory a thousand years earlier. Unfortunately, the name of whichever ancient Babylonian first cracked the theorem has been lost to history, so Pythagoras gets all the credit.

Fine. Shall we get on with the sum?

Sure. You see, this is the kind of fun that calculators deprive us of! Now, we've already multiplied the 6 in 396 by each digit of the 184, so we can forget about it now. We've carried the 9 from the third calculation, and we add to it 9 x 1 and 3 x 8, giving us 42. We should now have an answer that ends with 2864, just waiting for one last calculation.

Carry the 4, and add 3 x 1, and we're done. 396 times 184 is 72,864.[*]

Hooray!

And with a bit of practice, you can do that almost as quickly as any calculator! So, for one last example, let's do the eight-digit-number-by-eight-digit-number I mentioned earlier. In each calculation laid out below, there's a digit from the first number (27562946) multiplied by a digit from the second (72519463), in the same last-to-first sequence as before.

Calculation		Answer	digits
6x3		= 18	8
1 + 6x6 + 4x3		= 49	9
4 + 6x4 + 4x6 + 9x3		= 79	9
7 + 6x9 + 4x4 + 9x6 + 2x3		= 137	7
13 + 6x1 + 4x9 + 9x4 + 2x6 + 6x3		= 121	1
12 + 6x5 + 4x1 + 9x9 + 2x4 + 6x6 + 5x3		= 186	6
18 + 6x2 + 4x5 + 9x1 + 2x9 + 6x4 + 5x6 + 7x3		= 152	2
15 + 6x7 + 4x2 + 9x5 + 2x1 + 6x9 + 5x4 + 7x6 + 2x3		= 234	4
23 +	4x7 + 9x2 + 2x5 + 6x1 + 5x9 + 7x4 + 2x6	= 170	0

---

[*] Fermat's Last Theorem is another famous theorem that spins off from Pythagoras's – it says that $a^n + b^n = c^n$ can never be true where a, b and c are whole numbers and n is any number greater than 2. There are plenty of books about the attempts of mathematicians to prove the theorem over the last three hundred years or so, but none of them really gets to grips with the issue of why we call it his Last theorem, when he probably wrote it thirty years or so before he died. It wasn't discovered until after his death, scribbled in the margin of one of his books along with the helpful note that there is a remarkable proof that the margin didn't have enough space for him to write, but that doesn't make it his last theorem if you ask me.

Some people call it Fermat's Lost Theorem instead, probably by mistake resulting from mishearing someone clever talking about it, but I think that's a much more appropriate name, and I would like to use this footnote in chapter three of a book about funny party tricks to start a campaign to have Fermat's Last Theorem officially renamed. Who's with me?

17 +	9x7 + 2x2 + 6x5 + 5x1 + 7x9 + 2x4	= 190	0
19 +	2x7 + 6x2 + 5x5 + 7x1 + 2x9	= 95	5
9 +	6x7 + 5x2 + 7x5 + 2x1	= 98	8
9 +	5x7 + 7x2 + 2x5	= 68	8
6 +	7x7 + 2x2	= 59	9
5 +	2x7	= 19	9
1		= 1	1

And there you have it! The answer is 1,998,850,042,617,998. Call it two thousand billion[*], give or take.

Okay, how long does it take the best mental calculators to do that in their heads?

The current record (using the writing-down-one-digit-at-a-time method described above) is ten eight-digit by eight-digit multiplications in 13 minutes exactly, by Mohammed Seghir Saïd. Or if eight-by-eight is still a bit scary for you, try ten five-by-five mental multiplications in three minutes, six seconds, as set by Jan van Koningsveld in 2006.

The powers that be don't recognise records for doing just one calculation any more, because some are a lot easier to do than others, and one of these days the random number generator is going to give us 10000000 x 10000000 and some lucky calculator will come up with the answer in half a second (it's 100000000000000). But in the nineteenth century, a German called Zacharias Dase calculated an eight-digit-by-eight-digit multiplication in his head in 54 seconds, and for an encore, a 100-digit-by-100-digit multiplication in eight and three quarter hours. And this was before electronic calculators were invented, so it was really comparatively useful to be able to multiply long numbers in your head.

'Useful'? What possible reason could anybody ever have to need to multiply two hundred-digit numbers together?

---

[*] Some people say a billion is 1,000,000,000 (a thousand millions). Others, me included, say it's 1,000,000,000,000 (a million millions). That's because a billion is a million millions, or a million squared, hence the 'bi' in the name. A trillion is a million cubed, or 1,000,000,000,000,000,000 (that's a one with 18 zeroes after it). The way to remember the number of noughts is to multiply the number before the "illion" (bi, tri etc) by six. So an octillion is a 1 with 48 zeroes after it. But most people nowadays call a thousand million a 'billion', and who am I to argue? If you want to be pedantic, you can call a thousand million a 'milliard'. But don't expect anyone to understand you.

Well, maybe useful isn't the right word. Impressive, though! I bet lots of people thought Zacharias was clever.*

---

* There have been enough mathematical facts in this chapter's footnotes. Here's something different that you can use to change the subject if you find yourself dragged into a mathematical conversation and you've already used those killer lines about Pythagoras and Fermat – in Thailand, it's traditional to wear a different colour of clothing for each day of the week. Red on Sunday, yellow on Monday, pink on Tuesday, green on Wednesday, orange on Thursday, blue on Friday and purple on Saturday.

How To Memorise Numbers

Why would I want to memorise numbers?

Well, I'm not claiming that it's a skill that will benefit you enormously in real life. This isn't the kind of technique that you'd want to use to memorise a four-digit PIN number[*], but it's a natural kind of follow-on from the chapter on How To Memorise A Pack Of Cards, and it's very impressive if you can reel off pi to 1000 decimal places or more on demand.

Do I need to know the card thing before I do this?

Not necessarily, but it helps. You do need to read the parts of that chapter about journeys, and preferably also the parts about associating images with the cards, because we're going to do exactly the same thing with numbers. The only difference is that instead of the card suit providing our consonant sound, we're going to use something called the Major System to turn the numbers into sounds.

Who is Major?

The system is named after a guy called Major Beniowski (Major was his first name, not his rank. It was a fairly common name at one time, although it probably wasn't his original name, he having come from Poland), who didn't invent it. He was a famous mnemonist in London in the mid-19th century, or if not famous as such he was made fun of repeatedly in "Punch" magazine, which is as close to famous as it gets.

Who did invent it, then?

We should probably credit Johann-Just Winckelmann, also known for some reason as Stanislaus Mink von Wennsshein, the 17th-century writer with introducing the basic system, although various other people have tinkered with it over the years. And of course this tinkering is still going on today as everyone who learns memory techniques starts adding little refinements. The Major System should really be called the Group Effort System, if you ask me.

---

[*] The N in PIN stands for 'Number', so what I just said there was Personal Identification Number number. You can point this out to people who say that, if you want to be clever.

And how does the Major system work?

Like this:

1 = t/d
2 = n
3 = m
4 = r
5 = l
6 = g/j
7 = k
8 = h/f/v/th
9 = b/p
0 = s/z

The first thing to do, obviously, is to remember the letter associations. They're designed to be easy – a '1' looks a bit like a 't', 'n' has two vertical lines and 'm' has three, and so on. It takes a little bit of effort, but once you've got it cracked, you won't forget it. It's like riding a bike. Any time you see the number 4 you'll find yourself thinking 'rrrrr'.[*]

So we're going to use this to create images for two-digit numbers, the same as we did for the cards, using the Major-System letter for the first digit, and the vowel sound from the previous chapter for the second digit. You'll remember that those go like this:

1 = 'a'
2 = 'e'
3 = 'i'
4 = 'o'
5 = 'u'
6 = 'A'
7 = 'E'
8 = 'I'

---

[*] Some people like to say that the only two words in the English language that contain all five vowels, once only, in the correct order, are 'facetious' (meaning joking, or humorous) and 'abstemious' (meaning abstaining or exercising moderation). Since the internet came along, many other words fitting this pattern have been suggested, among them 'arsenious', 'annelidous', 'arterious', 'acheilous' and 'anemious'. And that's just the ones that start with A.

Rather than trying to list all the hundreds of words that actually have all five vowels, only once, in the correct order, the way to be clever here is to say "But what about 'facetiously' and 'abstemiously'?"

9 = 'O'
0 = 'U' or 'oo'

This way, if you've already created images for cards, you've got the images for forty out of the hundred possible two-digit combinations already prepared – 01 to 09 will be the same as the ace to nine of spades, and 00 the same as the ten of spades, the digits starting with 1 will match the diamonds, the 7s the clubs and the 8s the hearts.*

So I have to think up sixty more objects or people now?

'Fraid so. But it's not too difficult. Here are a few suggestions for the remaining two-digit combinations

20 (nU) – noose, nuke, Newton	40 – root, ruler, rooster	60 – goose, jukebox, Goofy
21 (na) – gnat, napkin, nan	41 – rat, rack, rabbit	61 – gasmask, jam, Jan
22 (ne) – net, neck, Ned	42 – wreck, relic, referee	62 – gecko, jester, Greg
23 (ni) – knickers, nib, Nick	43 – rib, rickshaw, rip	63 – giraffe, gig, Jill
24 (no) – knot, nozzle, Norris	44 – rock, robin, Ross	64 – gondola, goggles, jockey
25 (nu) – nut, nugget, nun	45 – rum, rug, Russell	65 – gun, jug, judge
26 (nA) – nail, nature, Nathan	46 – razor, railing, Ray	66 – gate, jade, Jake
27 (nE) – knee, kneeler, Nemo	47 – reel, reed, Rhys	67 – jeep, gearstick, geek
28 (nI) – knight, knife, ninepins	48 – rice, rifle, writer	68 – guide, geiger counter, Guy
29 (nO) – nose, notebook, gnome	49 – rose, roll, roach	69 – goat, joker, Joe

---

* Some people like to say that the nursery rhyme "Ring a ring o' roses" is about the bubonic plague, but there isn't actually any convincing evidence that this is true. It probably evolved from a dance song, like the lyrics would suggest. Contrary to what people who support this theory say, the plague didn't cause red rings on the skin, or sneezing – the main symptoms were swollen glands and black patches, hence 'black death'. But the plague-origin story has really caught on over the years, and often gets repeated by people who are trying to be clever. Here's your chance to set them straight.

30 (mU) – moose, moon, music	50 – loo, loot, Lulu	90 – boot, bouquet, booze
31 (ma) – map, mag, Matt	51 – lamb, ladder, Larry	91 – bat, balloon, baboon
32 (me) – melon, metal, Meg	52 – letter, lemon, Lenny	92 – berry, bed, Becker
33 (mi) – mint, mirror, Millie	53 – lift, lips, lily	93 – bin, bib, Bill
34 (mo) – moss, mop, Morris	54 – lorry, log, lock	94 – bomb, box, Bob
35 (mu) – mug, mummy, mud	55 – luggage, lung, lucky	95 – bus, button, book
36 (mA) – mace, mate, major	56 – laser, ladle, lake	96 – bear, baby, baker
37 (mE) – meal, meat, Mimi	57 – leek, leaf, Lisa	97 – bee, bean, beagle
38 (mI) – mime, milestone, Mike	58 – lime, lighter, Liza	98 – bison, bike, bible
39 (mO) – mower, mole, Mo	59 – loaf, logo, Lothar	99 – boat, bone, bowl

Any helpful hints?

I'm glad you asked. I'd suggest going for a roughly equal split between people and objects, to make sure that all the images are distinct from each other, and to make for more interesting scenarios when you put them together to memorise long numbers.[*]

So now we're going to do the same thing with numbers as we did with cards. Let's start with pi.

Pie? I'm not hungry, thanks.

Pi. Or π[†] if you want to be Greek about it. The mathematical constant which is also, for no reason anyone can remember, the classic test of

---

[*] 'Orchestra' is an anagram of 'carthorse'.
[†] π, if you don't remember learning about it at school, is the number you get when you divide the circumference of a circle by the diameter. If you really didn't learn anything at school, you might also need to know that 'circumference' means the length of the line that makes up the circle if you broke it somewhere and laid it out in a flat line to measure it. 'Diameter' means the length of a straight line drawn from any

memory. Being able to recite pi to a thousand decimal places is a sure-fire way to make people think you're clever. It starts like this: 3.14159265358. If we break this up into two-digit pairs, we have 31, 41, 59, 26, 53, 58. So in the first location on your journey you might have a mat (31) hiding a rat (41), which might be planning to go to the next location and steal a loaf of bread (59) from Nathan (26), who might leave it unattended while he goes along to the next location to take the lift (53) to get his lighter (58).

More! More!

Wow, you're unusually excitable today. Okay, here's pi to a thousand decimal places! Memorising this lot will take a lot of journeys, and probably a lot of time, but it's worth it for the looks of amazement it will generate when you recite it. The very best memorisers can memorise a thousand random digits in about half an hour, but there's no need to hurry with pi. Take your time and make sure those images are clear and fixed in your brain.

3.1415926535897932384626433832795028841971693993751058209749445923078164062862089986280348253421170679821480865132823066470938446095505822317253594081284811174502841027019385211055596446229489549303819644288109756659334461284756482337867831652712019091456485669234603486104543266482133936072602491412738

point on the circle through the exact centre to the other side. Or how high the circle would be if you stood it on its side.

Some people will tell you that pi is equal to 22 divided by 7, but this isn't true. 22 divided by 7 is 3.142857142857142857142857 and so on like that repeating 142857 forever. Memorising that number is really, really easy. Memorising pi is a lot harder, because it goes on and on forever as a string of totally random numbers with no pattern or repetition.

There is a super-computer in Japan dedicated to calculating pi to more and more decimal places every day. At the time of writing, it had got up to about five billion places [see page 21 – the people in charge of the computer say 'five trillion'.]

It is possible to mathematically prove that pi is both irrational (can't be expressed as one whole number divided by another) and transcendental (goes on forever with no pattern or repetition), but the proof is long, complicated and the kind of thing that you need to be a professor of mathematics to understand. Or so I'm told by professors of mathematics. It's possible that it's really simple and they just don't want to tell me so I'll think they're clever.

7245870066063155881748815209209628292540917153 6436
7892590360011330530548820466521384146951941511 6094
3305727036575959195309218611738193261179310511 8548
0744623799627495673518857527248912279381830119 4912
9833673362440656643086021394946395224737190702 1798
6094370277053921717629317675238467481846766940 5132
0005681271452635608277857713427577896091736371 7872
1468440901224953430146549585371050792279689258 9235
4201995611212902196086403441815981362977477130 9960
5187072113499999983729780499510597317328160963 1859
5024459455346908302642522308253344685035261931 1881
7101000313783875288658753320838142061717766914 7303
5982534904287554687311595628638823537875937519 5778
1857780532171226806613001927876611195909216420 1989*

Well, I've memorised it! Am I a world record holder now?

Not quite. The world record, held by Akira Haraguchi of Japan, currently stands at 100,000 decimal places, recited without error. It took him about sixteen hours to say all those numbers.

If you're really serious about memorising more than a thousand digits, it's probably best to expand the memory system you're using. The one taught in this chapter uses only a hundred different images – meaning that each one will occur an average of five times in a random thousand-digit number. Using a system of a thousand images – one for each three-digit combination – takes more advance preparation, but makes it a lot easier to memorise very long numbers. See the final chapter of this book for a brief guide to more advanced techniques!

My brain's still hurting after all that pi, thank you very much. Can we do something else now?

Okay. Turn the page, and see what wonders await!†

---

* See that bit, 762 digits after the decimal point, where it goes 999999? That is the only point in the first two hundred thousand digits where the same number repeats six times in a row. Pi has a few pretty patterns scattered through that mass of random digits – my favourite bit is where it goes 559555955 at 18,350 digits after the decimal point, which is less than a thousand digits after the 00000 at position 17,534. Little things like that are what really makes memorising pi fun!

† Dr Dionysius Lardner (1793 – 1859) was a well-known professor of natural history and astronomy, a brilliant mathematician and physicist who in the course of his life also found the time to work as a solicitor and a chaplain as well as writing numerous books on metaphysics, steam engines, calculus and geometry and spending several

years hiding in America after eloping with the wife of an army captain. He was a great guy all round, so it's unfortunate that his major claim to fame was announcing authoritatively that certain things were impossible.

"Rail travel at high speed is not possible," he noted in the early days of steam engines, "because passengers, unable to breathe, would die of asphyxia." He also proved that a steamship couldn't cross the Atlantic without running out of all the coal it could carry, less than two years before the first one did just that. He said the idea was as ridiculous as travelling to the moon.

How To Win At Blackjack

Can you do that Rain Man thing where you count cards in a casino and win millions of dollars?

No. I'm pretty sure nobody can do that. Although I've never even seen Rain Man, so I'm not sure exactly what happens in it.

You should. It's a good film.

Okay, I'll do my best to see it some time. Anyway, there is such a thing as counting cards, although it's not as glamorous or guaranteed to be successful as it seems in the movies.*

Okay, fair enough. So... what is blackjack?

The game that the casinos call 'blackjack' is known where I come from as 'pontoon', and some people like to call it 'twenty-one'. The rules are simple, and I'll explain them very briefly for the benefit of anyone who's never played the game before. Feel free to skip the next paragraphs if you already know it.

The aim of the game is to get a higher score than the dealer, without going over 21 points. You can ignore the other players (unless you're counting cards, which we'll come to in a moment). The competition is just you against the dealer. At the start of the game, the players and the dealer are each given two cards. Numbered cards score as many points as they have pips – the twos are worth two, the threes are worth three, and so on. Suits don't matter in blackjack. Jacks, Queens and Kings are all worth ten. Aces can count as either one or eleven, whichever makes the best score for you.

The players can then choose whether to take another card ('hit' or 'twist') or stick with just the cards they have ('stand' or 'stick'). You can keep taking cards, one at a time, until you decide to stop, or until your score goes over 21 ('break' or 'bust') in which case you lose. When all the players have finished, the dealer also hits or stands, and then all the

---

* The three longest-reigning kings in English history were all the third of their name – Henry III reigned for 56 years, Edward III for 50 and George III for 60. James I tends to be missed off this list – he was king of Scotland for 58 years, but only king of England as well for the last 22. The longest-reigning monarch of either gender or country, of course, was Victoria (the first and only), notching up 64 years. At the time of writing, Elizabeth II is at 58 years and still going strong.

players who have beaten the dealer win the amount of money they staked on the hand, the players who scored the same as the dealer get their stake back, and the players who scored lower than the dealer lose their money. If you and the dealer both bust, you still lose your money.

It's a simple game.* When you play in casinos, there are a few other things you need to know. If you are dealt a ten-card and an ace, a natural 21 ('blackjack'), you win more money (unless the dealer has a 21 too). This is nice, but of course it's not something you can control, so it won't be mentioned here again.

The dealer hits and stands according to fixed rules which will be written on the blackjack table. They don't get to choose whether to hit or stand based on what the players have scored. Normal practice in casinos is for dealers to be forced to hit any score of 16 or below, and stand on 17 or higher. One of the dealer's cards is visible to players from the start of the game, the other is hidden. This helps guide the players on whether to hit or stand.

If the dealer's face-up card is an ace, they offer you the chance to take out 'insurance' against the possibility that they have a blackjack. This involves betting a further half of your stake and getting your money back if the dealer does have a 21. Statistically speaking, taking insurance is never a good idea in normal non-card-counting play.

Players who are dealt two cards worth the same number of points can choose to 'split' them – put down another stake of the same value and have two hands, one with each of the cards. You choose to hit or stand with each hand separately.

Players can also choose to 'double down' – put down another stake of the same value as the original one and take exactly one more card. This, obviously, doubles your winnings if you beat the dealer, but doubles your losses if you lose.

---

* The youngest King of England was Henry VI, who became King at the age of nine months. James III of Cyprus holds the world record, though – he became King while still in the womb, in 1743. James was the only child of James II and his queen, Catherine, but if he had had an older sister, there would have been a fascinating situation – the unborn child would have been King if it was a boy, but the older sister would have been Queen if the unborn baby had been a girl, but since it wasn't possible to tell the sex of a child before birth in those days, nobody would have known who the monarch was!

Okay, I already know how to play. How do I win?

First off, it helps to know that it really is possible to win money at blackjack in casinos. The odds are tilted in favour of the dealer, but only very slightly. You have a much greater chance of winning money at blackjack than you do at roulette, craps or fruit machines. Casinos mainly include blackjack tables because they're traditional, and because they lure customers in to lose money on the more profitable games.

The other important thing about blackjack is that it isn't completely about random chance. If you know the basic rules of what to play in every situation, you have a big advantage over the uninformed player. Card-counting is less important than the following strategy tips.[*]

Know what to play based on the cards in your hand and the dealer's card that's showing. Many people have worked hard at calculating the odds for each situation, and some of these people even agree with each other some of the time. You should have no trouble finding detailed breakdowns of correct play for all variants of the rules and however many packs of cards the dealer has shuffled together (casinos vary between one and six packs). The table on the next page contains what I believe is the best way to go about playing if you only want to learn one table for any variation of rules.

It may look daunting at first, but it's all quite logical and it isn't that difficult to remember everything on it.

---

[*] It's not true that water spins clockwise in one hemisphere and anticlockwise in the other when draining out of a sink or toilet. There is such a thing as the Coriolis effect, but it affects the direction that tornadoes and big things like that spin in. Water will drain out in either direction in either hemisphere, depending on the shape of the sink or toilet in question.

Your hand	Dealer's face-up card									
	2	3	4	5	6	7	8	9	10	A
8 or less	h	h	h	h	h	h	h	h	h	h
9	h	d	d	d	d	h	h	h	h	h
10	d	d	d	d	d	d	d	d	h	h
11	d	d	d	d	d	d	d	d	d	d
12	h	h	s	s	s	h	h	h	h	h
13	s	s	s	s	s	h	h	h	h	h
14	s	s	s	s	s	h	h	h	h	h
15	s	s	s	s	s	h	h	h	h	h
16	s	s	s	s	s	h	h	h	h	h
17 or more	s	s	s	s	s	s	s	s	s	s
Ace & 2	h	h	h	d	d	h	h	h	h	h
Ace & 3	h	h	h	d	d	h	h	h	h	h
Ace & 4	h	h	d	d	d	h	h	h	h	h
Ace & 5	h	h	d	d	d	h	h	h	h	h
Ace & 6	h	d	d	d	d	h	h	h	h	h
Ace & 7	s	d	d	d	d	s	s	h	h	h
Ace & 8	s	s	s	s	s	s	s	s	s	s
Ace & 9	s	s	s	s	s	s	s	s	s	s
Two Aces	x	x	x	x	x	x	x	x	x	x
Two 2s	h	h	x	x	x	x	h	h	h	h
Two 3s	h	h	x	x	x	x	h	h	h	h
Two 4s	h	h	h	h	h	h	h	h	h	h
Two 5s	d	d	d	d	d	d	d	d	h	h
Two 6s	x	x	x	x	x	h	h	h	h	h
Two 7s	x	x	x	x	x	x	h	h	h	h
Two 8s	x	x	x	x	x	x	x	x	x	x
Two 9s	x	x	x	x	x	s	s	s	s	s
Two 10s*	s	s	s	s	s	s	s	s	s	s

h = Hit   s = Stand   d = Double down   x = Split

---

* 'Septal' is a word meaning 'relating to a septum', and unless you suffer from septal panniculitis or a ventricular septal defect, you're not likely to ever need to use it. But it is an interesting word in that it has only six letters, but six other words that are anagrams of it – palest, pastel, petals, plates, pleats and staple.

How can I remember all that?

It helps if you understand the reasoning behind it.[*] The first thing to bear in mind is that of the 52 cards in a pack, 16 of them are worth ten. So you're more likely to get a ten-card than any other value. Which means that if the dealer's face-up card is an 8, for example, the total they are most likely to have is 18. This gives you a guideline to aim for.

A very important rule is that the dealer keeps hitting until they reach 17 or more, and then they will stand. Hitting a total of 16 is dangerous, because only an ace, two, three, four or five will avoid going bust – five of the thirteen possible cards. Because of this, and the large number of ten-cards in the pack, the odds of the dealer going bust based on each face-up card work out like this:

2 – 35%	3 – 38%	4 – 40%	5 – 43%	6 – 42%
7 – 26%	8 – 24%	9 – 23%	10 – 24%	A – 17%

In other words, if the dealer is showing a 2, 3, 4, 5 or 6, they are much more likely to bust than if they're showing a higher card. Which is why the chart on the previous page advises you to stand with a total of 12-16 against a low face-up card and hit the same total against a high card. Being dealt a total between 12 and 16 makes it unlikely that you will win, but standing and hoping the dealer goes bust will work 43% of the time against a face-up 5.

The only exception to that rule is if you're dealt a 12 – there, while a ten-card will bust you, any other card will make your score a bit better, so the odds favour hitting a 12 against a face-up 2 or 3. But not a 4, 5 or 6.

Apart from that, you just need to remember to stand on anything 17 or over, and (obviously) hit anything under 12, because it's impossible to go bust with an extra card on top of 11 or less.

The rules of when to double down are also easy to remember – always double down if you're dealt an 11 (the chances of getting a 10-card to make 21 are good), double down on a 10 if the dealer is showing

---

[*] It is not true that right-handed people live longer than left-handed people. According to studies, the only time in history when hand preference made a difference to lifespan was in times of war, when lefties were more likely to be killed because they were handicapped by using weapons designed for right-handed people. The most extensive study of lifespan based on hand preference was done using cricket players, because their hand preference is always recorded.

anything but a 10 or an ace, double down on a 9 if the dealer is showing a bad face-up card (3 to 6).*

Then there are the hands where you have an ace. Since aces count as either one or eleven, an ace and a seven can be eight or eighteen (known as a 'soft 18'). This means that doubling down and taking an extra card gives you more chance of improving your hand than with a 'hard' total, because there is no chance of going bust. So the rule is to always stand on a soft 19 or 20, always hit a soft 13-17, and hit a soft 18 only if the dealer is showing a 9 or more. Which is easy to remember if you just bear in mind that the dealer's hidden card is most likely to be a ten.

The pattern for when the odds say it's a good idea to double down is easy to remember too – with ace-2 and ace-3 you double against a 5 and 6, with ace-4 and ace-5 you double against a 4, 5 and 6, with ace-6 and ace-7 you double against a 3, 4, 5 and 6. It's easy to remember that little step-shape on the chart (you might recall from the memory chapters of this book that thinking visually is the best way to remember something).

And if you have a pair, you just need to decide whether to split it (if you don't split it, you obviously do the same thing that you would with a non-pair hand making the same total. There are only a handful of rules to learn here.

Firstly, always split aces and eights (2, 12 and 16 are terrible starting totals to have, 11 or 8 is much better), and never split fours, fives and tens (8, 10 and 20 are very good totals to be dealt, and splitting them up can never be a good thing).

The others are probably easiest to learn by rote – split twos and threes against a 4, 5, 6 and 7. Split sixes for any face-up card 6 or less, sevens with any face-up card 7 or less. And finally, split nines for any face-up card 6 or less.

Okay, I sort of know all that. But if you know how to count cards, you don't need that stuff, right?

Sorry, but you do. You're never going to make any money from blackjack if you don't know the basic strategy outlined on the previous pages. Serious card-counters, in fact, have memorised the various

---

* In a standard pack of playing cards, all the male picture cards have moustaches, except the King of Hearts and the Jack of Clubs.

different combinations of house rules and numbers of decks in a lot more detail than that, and will simply follow these strategies at least three-quarters of the time, without factoring any changes from card-counting.*

You're making card-counting sound a lot less magic than I thought.

Sorry, but that's the way of the world. To make up for it, here's an introduction to how to do it!

The basic principle of card-counting is that the player's chance of winning a hand gets higher proportionately to the number of high cards remaining in the deck. The things that the player can do but the dealer can't, like splitting and doubling down, are more likely to generate more money for the player if the pack has more tens in it. Likewise, the chances of the dealer going bust slowly rise if the deck has a high proportion of tens, and fall if there is a high proportion of twos, threes and fours waiting to be dealt.

What card-counters do is keep track of how many of each value of cards have already been dealt, and so calculate whether their chance of winning a hand has increased or decreased. The simplest way to take advantage of card-counting is to bet larger amounts when you know the deck is full of high cards, and smaller amounts when it isn't. The truly obsessed with blackjack can also recalculate the hit-or-stand tables for each hand based on the new odds of beating the dealer.

The most basic card-counting system, which practically everybody knows, is to assign one point to each 2, 3, 4, 5 and 6, zero points to each 7, 8 or 9, and minus one point for each 10, J, Q, K and Ace. As the cards are dealt out and played, just add the running total up in your head, and if it gets to a high positive value (meaning there are lots of high cards still to come), start betting more heavily, if it gets to a high negative, reduce your bets or move to another table and start again.

There are many more complicated variations on this system, and they generally all claim to give the best possible results. For example, the following should give a slightly more accurate representation of the 'value' of the remaining cards:

---

* Tarot cards, despite what fortune-tellers will tell you, were invented in Europe in the 15th century, and were intended solely for playing card games with. They have only been used for fortune-telling since the late 18th century.

2	3	4	5	6	7	8	9	10	A
+1	+1	+2	+2	+2	+1	0	-1	-2	0

The count needs to be adjusted bearing in mind the number of cards left in the dealer's "shoe". A lot of casinos use up to eight packs, all shuffled together (and only deal out roughly two-thirds of them before reshuffling and starting again), so obviously dealing four or five sixes out of that doesn't make so much difference. So you need to divide the running total of your count by the approximate number of decks left in the shoe to get the true count.

Feeling ambitious? Using the number-memory techniques described in the first chapter of this book, it's also possible to keep a mental count of exactly how many of each value of card has come out so far. If you've worked through that chapter already, you should have already got in your head a mental image for each two-digit number from 00 to 99. Let's play through a couple of hands of blackjack and see how we can use those mental images to our advantage.

Three players and a dealer are sitting at the table (well, the dealer's standing up, as is the custom in casinos). They're using two packs shuffled together. The dealer's face card is the King of diamonds. Player 1, let's call him Bob, has the four of spades and the five of clubs. Player 2, let's call her Carol, has the three of spades and the nine of spades. Player 3, that's you, has the eight of clubs and the ace of spades.[*]

Ooh, good hand, right?

$$10 - ?$$

$$4 - 5 \qquad\qquad 3 - 9 \qquad\qquad 8 - A$$

Right. But a complicated hand for card-counting. That's one each of ace, three, four, five, eight, nine and ten (remember, the picture cards all count as ten). We can remember these as 11, 13, 14, 15, 18, 19 and 10. Which, using your mental images, you might remember as Dad in a digger, digging up a doll and a duck to give to a diver with a doughnut by a dune.

---

[*] The dodo was declared extinct in 1681. It was only ever known to live on the small island of Mauritius, and the first Portuguese sailors to discover it, in the early 16th century, reported that it didn't taste very good.

Bob hits his nine to get the three of clubs, mutters something foul under his breath, hits again to get the five of spades, sighs, and sticks with his seventeen. He knows his basic strategy gives him the highest chance of winning that way, but he also knows that his chance of winning is still pretty low. Carol hits her twelve, gets the six of spades and sticks with her eighteen. You have the sense to stick with your soft 19, and the dealer turns her card over to reveal a nine of spades.

10 – 9

| 4 – 5 – 3 – 5 | 3 – 9 – 6 | 8 – A |

So you get your money back, whereas Bob and Carol have lost theirs. All this time, you've been updating your mental totals. We've now got two fives, so the duck has turned into a nut (the image for 25), two threes, so the digger has turned into a pair of knickers (23), and two nines, giving us a gnome instead of a doughnut. We've also got a six, bringing Dale Winton to join the party. Now Dad, wearing knickers, is giving a doll and a nut to Dale and the diver, watched by a gnome on the dune.*

We play another hand.

4 – ?

| 7 – 6 | 5   2 | A – 6 |

Which after some more sensible play turns out like this:

4 – 10 – 10

| 7 – 6 | 5 – 2 – 9 | A – 6 – 8 |

And since you doubled down on your ace-six, like the chart tells you to do, you won double your stake. Well done! And while you've been playing, your mental picture has become 21, 12, 23, 24, 35, 36, 17, 28, 39, 30 – Nan in a deckchair waving her knickers in a knot at a mummy with a mace followed by a DJ sticking a knife in a mower owned by a moose. You get the idea. Keep modifying the picture every time you see a new card, and you'll have a count in your head of exactly how many of each card you get. When the count of tens gets over 10 (as it quickly will

---

* When he was originally created in 1938, Superman couldn't fly, just jump really, really high. He didn't gain the ability to fly until 1944.

a lot of the time), start from one again and put one of your gambling chips inconspicuously in front of you to remind you you're on your second batch of tens.

Things go on like this and after another couple of deals, the count has got to 41, 52, 33, 74, 45, 36, 17, 48, 59, 60. Now you sit back and think about what this means. Since we're using two packs of cards shuffled together, that means there are eight of each value in the shoe. Except for the ten-cards, of which there are 32. The immediate thing that jumps out at you is that there have only been six tens. You would normally expect to see four times as many tens as other cards, which means that there are likely to be a lot of tens to come (which is very good news for the players).

Also, a lot of low cards have come out, especially the fours – there is only one four left in the shoe. If you find yourself in a situation where a four would be the best card (this kind of situation is sadly rare in blackjack), you'll know it's almost certainly not going to happen. But if the dealer ends up with a 16, she's almost certain to go bust with this distribution of cards in the pack. If the dealer's face-up card comes out as a five or six here, and you get a couple of low cards, you could double down in the reasonably certain expectation of winning.

So if I know this, can I quit my job and win a fortune at the casinos?

I wouldn't recommend trying. They call it gambling for a reason – even using the most perfect basic strategy and the most complicated card-counting system, the possibility still exists of losing every single hand. That's random chance for you. Much better to use these tricks to demonstrate your skills in friendly games with people you know, playing for matchsticks.*

---

* Big Ben, as well as being a nickname of mine that I dislike (please don't call me Big Ben if you meet me), is in fact the name of the bell in the clock tower at the Palace of Westminster. It is not the name of the tower, or the clock, despite common usage. The confusion came about because of the tradition of listening to Big Ben strike the hour on the radio in pre-television days. When you phrase it like that, naturally people assume Big Ben is the name of the tower.

Also of interest, the clock face on the tower has the hours marked in Roman numerals, but says 'IV' for four, instead of the 'IIII' that you will see on most clocks.

How To Get Into Mensa

Mensa?

One of the best ways to prove how clever you are is to join Mensa, the high-IQ society.[*] Although qualification for the society is just by getting a high score on an IQ test, anyone who can wave a Mensa membership card around tends to be taken as a leading authority on any subject, even if they know nothing about it. It's well worth the membership fee, just for that!

But don't you have to be a super-genius to get in?

Not really. The main reason why being a member is seen as proof of genius is not the difficulty of getting in (you don't actually have to be Einstein, strange as it may sound), but the small proportion of people who qualify for membership who actually join.

You need to score above 148 on Mensa's standard IQ test to be eligible to join the society. This score is achieved by 2% of the population, which means that of the 60,000,000 people in Britain, 1,200,000 could be in Mensa. More than a million! However, British Mensa only has 24,000 members at last count, so by joining, you give the impression of being in a very small minority of geniuses. 0.04% sounds a heck of a lot more impressive than 2%, doesn't it?

Okay, but I don't think I'm in the top 2% of the population, either.

Don't worry. In an ideal world, intelligence tests would be a pure measure of intelligence, requiring no underlying knowledge, making it impossible to prepare for a test, because you'd get the same IQ score every time. In the real world, it doesn't quite work like that. It's impossible to create a test that is based on pure natural intelligence, so for every IQ test you encounter, it helps to know a few little things. This chapter will teach a few things that might be helpful if you want to take the Mensa test.

---

[*] 'Mensa' is the Latin word for 'table'. Many people write it as 'MENSA' as if each letter stood for something, but they don't. The founder, Lance Ware, chose to call the society Mensa because it sounds like the Latin word for 'mind', which is 'mens', and because he envisaged a round-table society where geniuses come together on equal terms to talk about clever subjects.

Okay, where do we start?

Let's start with numbers, since so much of this book is about them. A lot of IQ puzzles give you a sequence of numbers and ask you to fill in the blanks, like this:*

1, 3, 6, 10, 15, _, 28

And any vaguely intelligent person should be able to work out that the answer is 21 (it increases by two, then three, then four, and so on). Yes, some IQ puzzles really are that easy. More often, though, they try to confuse you in one of only a few different ways.

Try this one:

1, 9, 3, 3, 5, 1, _

It's confusing at first glance, since it seems to go up and down, but if you look at every other number, you'll see that it goes 1, 3, 5, while the numbers in between go 9, 3, 1. In other words, it's two different progressions shuffled together, the first one increasing by two each time, the other one dividing by three. And the next in the sequence needs to be a 7. A lot of number puzzles in IQ tests are like this.

Generally, number sequence puzzles involve adding, subtracting or multiplying. Here's another example of the kind of puzzle you'll see very often:

1, 1, 2, 3, 5, 8, 13, _

Instead of increasing at a steady rate, what's happening here is that each number is the sum of the previous two numbers in the sequence – except the first, which is just 1, but you'll often find 'except' clauses like that in the answers.

---

* Queen Victoria is the great-great-grandmother of Queen Elizabeth II, and also the great-great-grandmother of Prince Philip. Thanks to all the intermarrying in the royal family over the centuries, practically all of Queen Elizabeth II's ancestors for the past hundred years were direct descendants of William the Conqueror, making him literally hundreds of her great-grandfathers.

The other thing that puzzle-writers usually assume you know is prime numbers.

What's a prime number?

You might remember from school that a prime number is a number that can only be divided by itself and 1 to give a whole number answer. So 4 isn't a prime number, because it can be divided by 2; 9 isn't a prime number because it can be divided by 3; but 11 is a prime number because it can't be divided by anything.[*]

You don't really need to know that. But to understand some number sequences, you need to know that the sequence of prime numbers goes like this: 1, 2, 3, 5, 7, 11, 13, 17, 19, 23, 29. You don't really need to know any more than that. Now a puzzle like this should be easy:

3, 4, 5, 7, 9, 13, _

Obviously, it's 15, because it's that list of prime numbers, with 2 added to each one.

Okay, test me!

Try these puzzles for size. There are a few more common tricks in them, intended to trip you up, but see if you can work them out without looking at the answers.

a) 2, 6, 18, 54, 162, _
b) 2, 12, 30, 56, 90, 132, _
c) 1, 3, 7, 15, 31, 63, _
d) -4, -3, -2, 0, 2, 6, 8, 12, 14, 18, _
e) 1, 1, 2, 2, 4, 2, 4, 2, _
f) 1, 3, 3, 6, 5, 9, 7, _
g) -3, 8, -15, 24, -35, _
h) a, c, f, j, o, _
i) 92, 84, 78, 616, _
j) 291, 232, 193, 175, 137, _
k) 31, 28, 31, 30, _
l) 1, 2, 3, 3, 7, 5, 15, 9, _, _

---

[*] The equator runs through the following countries – Ecuador, Colombia, Brazil, Gabon, Republic of the Congo, Democratic Republic of the Congo, Uganda, Kenya, Somalia and Indonesia.

What are the answers?

Well, I hope you at least gave them a try before turning the page. The answers are as follows:[*]

a) 2, 6, 18, 54, 162, **486** – it multiplies by three each time. It's not unusual to find puzzles that assume you can multiply 54 or 162 by three in your head. Get practicing with that mental arithmetic!

b) 2, 12, 30, 56, 90, 132, **182** – the gap between numbers increases by 8 each time.

c) 1, 3, 7, 15, 31, 63, **127** – another common sequence is powers of 2; 2, 4, 8, 16, 32 and so on. Here we've subtracted 1 from each number, to make it less obvious. Or, to look at it another way, each number is multiplied by two and subtract one to get the next in the sequence.

d) -4, -3, -2, 0, 2, 6, 8, 12, 14, 18, **24** – good old prime numbers again, this time with 5 subtracted from each one.

e) 1, 1, 2, 2, 4, 2, 4, 2, **4** – and this one is the difference between successive prime numbers.

f) 1, 3, 3, 6, 5, 9, 7, **12** – two different sequences alternating, one of them increases by 3 each time, the other by 2.

g) -3, 8, -15, 24, -35, **48** – just ignore the minus signs, they're obviously just appearing on alternate numbers. This is a simple sequence with the gap between numbers increasing by 2 each time.

h) a, c, f, j, o, **u** – another thing it's a real help to know is the number values of letters. A is the first letter of the alphabet, C is the third, F is the sixth, J is the tenth and you can see how this is working now, can't you?

i) 92, 84, 78, 616, **532** – this question is a real cheat. It's two alternating sequences, but they've been merged into one number. The first one goes 9, 8, 7, 6, 5, and the second goes 2, 4, 8, 16, 32.

---

[*] The Republic of the Congo and the Democratic Republic of the Congo are two neighbouring but separate countries, which have never been one combined big country like the old East and West Germany, or North and South Korea. The RC was a French colony, the DRC was Belgian.

j) 291, 232, 193, 175, 137, **1111** – and this is even more of a cheat. It's doing the same thing as the last one, but with descending and ascending sequences of prime numbers. 29, 23, 19, 17, 13, 11 and 1, 2, 3, 5, 7, 11. Always keep an eye out for that 1-2-3-5-7 pattern, it's a big clue.

k) 31, 28, 31, 30, **31** – this one isn't numbers at all, really. It's just the number of days in each month.

l) 1, 2, 3, 3, 7, 5, 15, 9, **31**, **17** – two sequences again, the first one you multiply by two and add one, the second you multiply by two and subtract one. Or, in each case, the difference between successive numbers multiplies by two each time. There are often different ways to get to the same answer.

Can I get into Mensa now?

Sorry, number sequences are just one of many kinds of puzzle you'll find in IQ tests. But they are a very useful exercise for getting your mind thinking the right way, so after that workout, the rest of the chapter should be easy!*

Other number puzzles you might encounter involve more complicated mathematics. A lot of the time, they involve the use of algebra. This kind of puzzle is frowned upon in serious IQ-testing circles, since it requires more underlying knowledge than the sequence puzzles, but you will still encounter a lot of them, even in the most serious and official of IQ tests.

For example, train A leaves station A and travels towards station B, 120 miles away, at 30 miles per hour, while at the same time train B leaves station B and travels at 60 miles per hour directly towards station A. How long will it be before the two trains crash into each other?

So to solve this puzzle, you need to work out that it's actually just a simple equation. You can see quickly enough that train A travels half a mile every minute, and train B covers one mile every minute. Since between them they travel exactly 120 miles, and B is going twice as fast as A, B will cover twice as much distance as A. A very basic bit of algebra or mental calculation will tell you that B will travel 80 miles and A will travel 40. And another little bit of maths will tell you that the journey takes 80 minutes.

---

* The first poet buried in Poets' Corner at Westminster Abbey was Geoffrey Chaucer, who died in 1400. But it didn't become Poets' Corner until a second poet, Edmund Spenser, was buried there too in 1599.

As another example, if 5 apples and 4 oranges cost 70p, and 7 apples and three oranges cost 85p, how much is one apple and one orange?*

It's like being back at school, isn't it? If you haven't had to do equations for a few years, get back in practice before taking an IQ test. If you're still at school, or if you're working as a greengrocer with a very unusual pricing system, this should be a lot easier, just because you're used to doing this kind of calculation.

You might be able to see at a glance that apples are 10p and oranges are 5p – the numbers in IQ tests are not normally difficult. But just in case you need a refresher course on turning it into algebra, $5x + 4y = 70$; $7x + 3y = 85$.

Multiplying by 3 and 4 to make the y values equal: $15x + 12y = 210$
$28x + 12y = 340$

Subtracting one from the other: $13x = 130$; $x = 10$.

Knowing how to do this, and expecting to need to do this, is a big advantage when doing puzzles.

Does it have to be numbers all the time?

Let's move on to word puzzles. These come in two basic kinds – the type where you need to know the meaning of the word, and the type where you don't. We'll look at the second kind first. As mentioned above, you will sometimes see number puzzles where numbers are disguised as letters. There are other ways in which puzzles can pretend to be word puzzles, like the following:

POTATO, BANANA, TOMATO, DONATE, LUCITE
Which word fits with the others?
a) CHEESE   b) HAVANA   c) CARROT   d) ACTIVE

The answer is nothing to do with what the words mean, it's b) HAVANA, because it has alternating consonants and vowels, like the words above. Here's another example:

---

* Also buried in Poets' Corner, although he wasn't a poet, is Thomas Parr, who allegedly lived to be 152 years old (1483-1635). But records of the first hundred years or so of his life are basically non-existent, so there seems good reason to doubt that he really was that old.

BAN, CAP, DAR, EAT, ___

Which word comes next in the list?
a) HAD   b) FAV   c) GET   d) JAB

If this comes along mixed in with word puzzles, you might forget the rules of sequences. It's obviously b), because the first letter is increasing alphabetically by one each time, and the last letter is increasing by two.*

So those are the kind of word puzzles that aren't really about words at all. But there can be other word puzzles like the following:

What four-letter word can be added to the end of all these words to make a new word each time? HEAD, BE, LIFE, FUR

The answer is 'LONG'. These puzzles are frowned upon even more sternly than the puzzles involving algebra, because they're much more a test of knowledge than of pure intelligence – they presuppose that you know of all the words being used. But you will still find them in tests, and all I can suggest is that you learn a few unusual words, just in case. A furlong is an eighth of a mile.

I knew that. Is that all the different kinds of puzzles?

Not by a long shot. But if you know those basic types, you can certainly increase your score on most IQ tests. The final kind of puzzle we're going to talk about here is the least easy to prepare for, the least reliant on underlying knowledge, and so the most popular with everybody except the people who have to create the puzzles (because it's a lot more work for them). They're known as 'Culture Fair' tests, and they generally consist of multiple choice odd-one-out or next-in-the-sequence puzzles involving funny shapes and patterns. Here are a few examples:

1)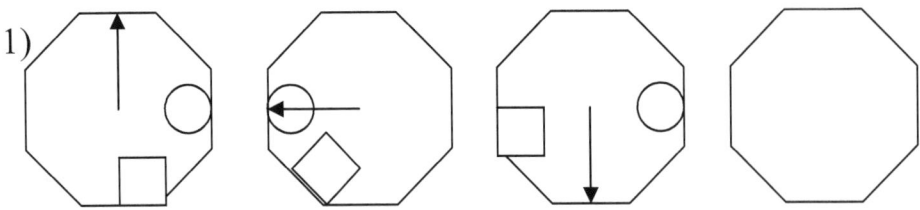

Fill in the blank octagon from the options below.

---

* 'Tmesis' means inserting one word into another compound word, as in 'un-flipping-believable', or 'well, halle-flaming-lujah'.

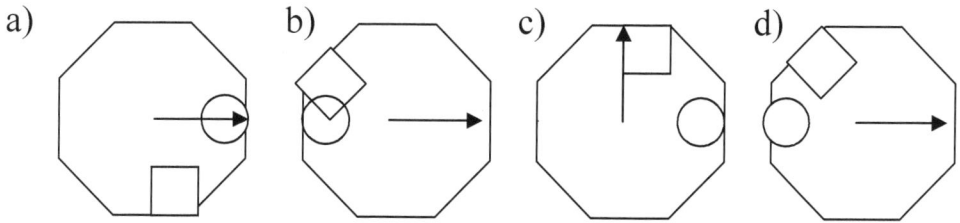

2) Which is the odd one out?*

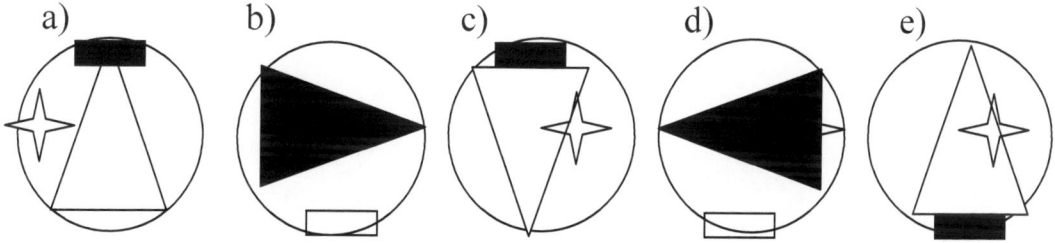

3) Which is the missing tile?

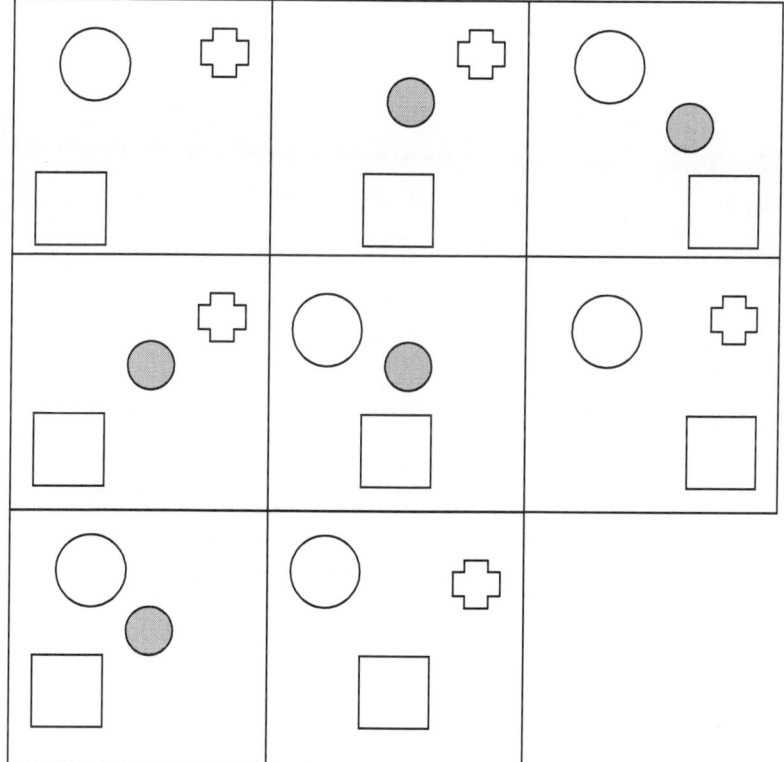

---

* Lobsters can live to be over a hundred years old, if they don't get eaten first. They also keep growing at a steady rate throughout their lives.

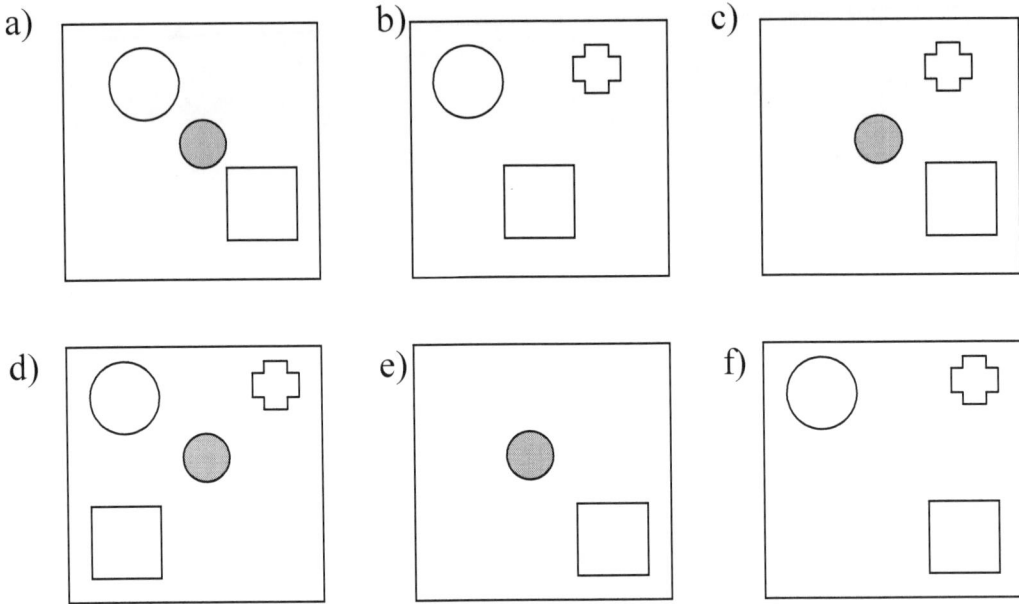

1) The answer is b). The shapes all move around the octagon in sequence, and it's just a matter of following them and working out where they will go next.

2) The answer is e). Again, everything is moving in sequence, and here some of the shapes are changing colours too. The black rectangle in e) is in the wrong place. Notice that in b), the star is hidden behind the triangle. This kind of trick is quite common in these puzzles.*

3) The answer is c). Here we have not only a square moving gradually from right to left in each row, but other shapes appearing and disappearing so that each row and each column contains two of each kind of shape. These puzzles invariably have multiple-choice answers, which can often be a big help – if you've worked out how the square moves, you can eliminate the two possible answers with the square in the wrong place, and study the others to see which fits the pattern best.

So now can I get into Mensa?

Well, I'd recommend practicing a little bit more before you try to join. There are many, many puzzle books in the shops, and many, many

---

* Another interesting thing about lobsters is that the left and right sides of their bodies can in rare cases be completely different colours, because they develop separately from each other.

websites full of free IQ puzzles, all of which will provide good practice for the kind of test you have to take when you join.

How do you join, anyway?

Write to Mensa, or contact them through their website, and they'll send you a little test to do at home. If you get a good score on this test, they'll invite you to come and take a supervised test somewhere, usually in a university or similar building, at various locations around the country or the world.

Get a high enough IQ score on that test, and you're in. Although you have to pay a membership fee. But remember, it's worth it for the admiration of your peers!*

---

* Most, but not all, lobsters are left-handed (that is, their left claw is larger than the right).

How To Not Play Chess

How to not play chess?

That's right. Perhaps the most universally-accepted measure of cleverness is the ability to play chess very well. If this book does what it's supposed to do and gives you a reputation among your family and friends of being "clever", people will probably just assume that you're really good at chess, because that's what clever people do. It certainly happens to me, and I'm terrible at the game.

So, if you find yourself in the same position, the best way to keep your reputation intact is not to play chess at all (because there really is no short cut to becoming a really good player, it takes years. Literally.), and this chapter gives a couple of suggestions for the best way to avoid playing chess – to play another, less well known, complicated strategy game, and encourage everyone else to play it too. There are lots of such games out there if you know where to look, and if you're the one who introduces it to everybody you play against, you should have no problem keeping that clever-person reputation going.

No, I meant that 'How To Not Play Chess' is a split infinitive, and really terrible grammar.

I realise that, but I don't really care. Can we get on with these games, now?*

Okay then. What's first?

Othello, aka Reversi

Why the two names?

The game of reversi was invented in 1880 by Lewis Waterman. It was argued that he had in fact just modified the rules of a game that had been invented a decade previously and passed it off as a new game, but reversi,

---

* Another useful grammatical point that nobody cares about is the 'rule' that you should never end a sentence with a preposition. Prepositions are words like 'with', 'at' and 'by', and although it's considered good form to phrase sentences in such a way that they don't end with them, it's not technically a hard-and-fast rule of grammar, and anyone who says it is is mistaken. So next time someone asks you "What are you looking at?", you don't need to reply "Actually, you should say 'At what are you looking?'"

unlike John W Mollett's 'annexation,' became quite popular in Victorian England.* Eventually people lost interest, and the game faded into obscurity until it was 'invented' again in Japan in the early 1970s by Goro Hasegawa. This time the new 'inventor' only made two incredibly minor changes to the rules, but it was still considered new enough to trademark the 'new' game as Othello, and get money from the sale of it.

Of course, the old name makes it very easy for people to get round the awkward legal things that come with using trademarked names, which is why if you want to play Othello on the internet, you'll find it being called reversi.

So how do you play?

It's very easy to learn the rules. The board is eight squares by eight squares, like a chess board. The pieces are all identical – they're discs which are white on one side and black on the other. One player is white, the other is black, and the aim is to make as many of the discs on the board as possible turn to your colour. To demonstrate, here's the start of a game. Games begin with four pieces already set up on the board, like this:

The player with the black pieces starts. He/she/it has to place a piece on the board so that a white piece is sandwiched on two opposite sides by black pieces.

So in the starting position, there are four places Black can play, marked with little numbers.

---

* Funnily enough, only a couple of years after Lewis Waterman invented reversi in England, another Lewis Waterman, no relation, invented the fountain pen in America. Well, actually he just improved on the design of the fountain pen so that it worked better, and successfully marketed it, just like his namesake did with reversi.

	1	●	2			
		●	●			
		3	●	o		

If Black chooses to play at position 1, the sandwiched white piece is flipped over and becomes black.

Now White has the choice of three moves to play – the sandwich can be horizontal, vertical or diagonal.

Wait a minute. Black plays first?

Yes. In practically every black-versus-white board game in the world, black plays first. Chess is just about the only game that does it differently. If you're going to become skilled at not playing chess, get used to playing first with the black pieces.*

So, to continue with the rules…

			1			
		o	o	o		
		o	o	o		
	●	o	o	o		
	o		●	●	●	

Here we are a bit further in the game. You can see that there have been ten moves made so far – once a piece has been put down, it stays there forever. It's Black's move, and he might choose to play at position 1. This would be a pretty bad move, for reasons we'll talk about in a moment, but it highlights another important rule of the game.

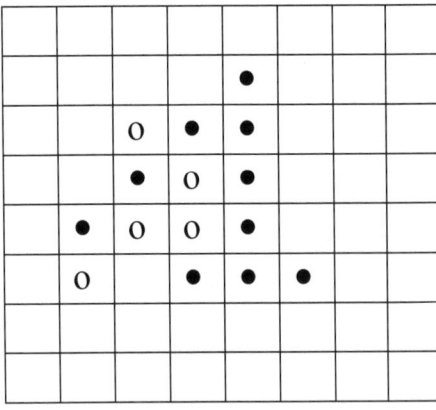

Black's move has flipped three white discs downwards and two diagonally, by trapping them between the disc played and those two black discs that were there already.
However, those three white discs in the middle, even though they are now trapped between black discs, remain white.

---

* When squirrels bury nuts for the winter, they don't remember where they put them. When winter comes, they dig randomly in the ground around where they live until they find something that they or another animal had buried.

So, as you can see, discs can be flipped in two or more directions at once, but only discs trapped by the disc placed on the board are flipped – there are no chain reactions.* You also don't get a choice as to whether to flip discs – there might be times when you would want to leave a disc your opponent's colour, but they have to be flipped if they're trapped between your disc and another of your colour.

o							
o		●	●	●			
o	●	●	●	●			
o	o	●	●	●	●		
o	●	o	●	●	●		
o	●	●	●	●	●		
o	●						

One more rule is worth knowing. Every move you play must flip at least one of your opponent's discs. If you can't play any move that traps an opponent's disc between two of yours, you skip a turn. Here, for example, it's Black's turn to play, but he can't play anywhere that captures any white discs, so White plays again.

This position illustrates some more very useful basic things to know about playing othello. Notice that White has a piece in the corner. Corners are the best squares to have a piece on, because once a disc is played there, it can never be flipped – it's impossible to play discs on two sides of it, because the corner squares don't squares on any two opposite sides! So rule one of playing well is to try to get discs of your colour in the corners. And naturally, rule two is to try not to play discs in the squares next to the corners, and allow your opponent to play there next.

And, following on from that, White's column of discs down the left hand side of the board can also never be flipped, because of the corner piece at one end of the line – if you think about it, you can see that there is no way to ever surround any of those discs.

This highlights another thing you need to know to be a good player of othello. White has nine discs on the board and Black has twenty, but White is in a much better position here. This isn't a freak situation. Generally speaking, in a game of othello, the player with fewer discs in the early stages is likely to win in the end. In the position above, for example, White has lots of choices of moves. He can play in such a way that Black has only one or two moves available, and thus force Black to play in a bad square, like the one next to a corner.

---

* The southern hemisphere equivalent of the northern lights, or aurora borealis, is called the aurora australis. Despite the name, it can only be seen in Antarctica, not Australia ('austral' means 'south' in Latin).

		3	O	●	4		
	7	6	●	O	1		
				2			
	9	8	5				

Let's play through a game and illustrate some of these points in action. Black here is a bad player who doesn't appreciate the strategy and tries to take as many discs as possible, White is a clever player who knows what he's doing. If you've got a board, you can follow the numbers and see what happens. Remember, Black goes first.*

	14	17			13		
		●	●	●	O		
12	●	●	●	O	●		
		15	O	16			
	●	●	●	11			
18		10					

Here we are after move 9. Black has just played into the square diagonally adjacent to the corner, which is the worst place you can possibly play. He did have a couple of other moves available, but White had so few discs, and they were so positioned in the middle of a sea of black, that soon enough Black would have been forced to make the bad move.

Notice that at one point White was reduced to just one disc, but was still completely in control of the game. Naturally, if you are reduced to zero discs, you lose, but it doesn't take much thinking to be sure that that doesn't happen.

23							
28	O	●			●		
27	26	●	●	●	●		
O	O	●	O	●	●		
20	19	O	●	O			
21	O	●	●	●	25		
O	22	24	O				

Without needing any real strategy more complex than taking as few discs as possible each move, White quickly arranges it so that he can play in the bottom left corner with move 18. Now that disc will remain white, and any white discs played next to it will remain white too. Black has more discs, but he's really in trouble here.

---

* Teddy bears were named after US President Theodore "Teddy" Roosevelt, and first sold in late 1902. Roosevelt had only been the President for a year – if William McKinley hadn't been assassinated, perhaps the cuddly toys would be known today as willy bears. 'Willy' meaning 'penis' was first recorded in 1905.

	29							
	●	30	31					
	o	●	●	32		●		
	o	o	●	●	●	●		
	o	o	o	●	●	●		
	o	o	o	o	●			
	o	o	o	o	●	●		
	o	o	o	o				

By move 28, Black has ended up forced to let White take control of that whole bottom corner, with no chance of ever turning any of those discs black again. Now Black can't play anywhere, so White plays again, and again, and now it's just a matter of filling the board with white discs as quickly as possible, by preventing Black from having a move.

	o							
	o	o	o					
	o	o	o	o		●		
	o	o	o	o	●	●		
	o	o	o	o	●	●		
	o	o	o	o	●			
	o	o	o	o	●	●		
	o	o	o	o				

White plays four moves in a row, and makes it perfectly clear, if it wasn't before, that Black is well and truly dead. There is now only one place he can play, next to the corner in the top left, and then White can play a string of moves once again and get rid of all Black's remaining discs. You can finish the game by yourself, I'm sure.

So, am I an expert at othello now?

No, there's a lot more to strategy than that, but if you just follow these basic principles, you've got a head start over most of the players in the world.[*]

In summary:

1) Try to take as few discs as possible.
2) Aim to reduce the number of moves your opponent is able to play.
3) Make sure not to let your opponent play to the corners.

Then, once you're comfortable with all that, look into more detailed strategy, play some good players, and become brilliant, if that's what you want. But this book isn't about becoming a grand master, it's about becoming clever.

---

[*] Everyone has heard of the Lincoln and Kennedy assassinations, but McKinley's seems to have been forgotten by history. It's possible that this is because the man who killed him was called Leon Czolgosz rather than a catchy name like John Wilkes Booth or Lee Harvey Oswald.

Well, that's all well and good, but how about a game that's more like chess?

Well, if that's your cup of tea, I recommend the second alternative in this chapter:

Xiangqi, aka Chinese Chess

Two names again?

Chinese Chess is a game from China, hence the name, that is related to chess, has pieces that move in the same way and shares a lot of the strategy. The two games diverged from a common ancestor thousands of years ago, and have taken on a life of their own. In China, the game is called Xiangqi, or Hsiang Ch'i if you prefer to use the old-fashioned way of representing Chinese characters in the Roman alphabet. Either way, it's pronounced shee-ang chi.[*]

What does it mean?

'Elephant game'. It's a sort of untranslatable Chinese joke that must have entertained the mediaeval Chinese players – the pieces that correspond to the bishops in western chess are called either elephants or chancellors, because the words sound identical in Mandarin Chinese. Incidentally, in ancient times, the bishops in western chess were elephants too, there being more elephants than bishops in ancient India, where the game originated. They were turned into bishops when the game came to mediaeval Europe, in order to make it more like the wars the western players were accustomed to.

Do I need to know how to play normal chess before I can play the Chinese kind?

Yes. Well, not really – obviously, you can learn to play Chinese chess without knowing the rules of western chess, and it might even be an advantage, avoiding the confusion caused by the slight differences. But if you're reading this book, which has a limited number of pages to introduce the game to you, then yes, you need to know chess. Because there are a lot of similarities, and I'm going to say things like 'it moves like a rook moves in chess' and assume you know what I mean.

---

[*] The only British Prime Minister to be assassinated was Spencer Perceval, in 1812. He was killed by John Bellingham.

I know how the pieces move in chess, but I'm a terrible player. Does that matter?

Not at all! You, in fact, are exactly the kind of person this section is aimed at. Soon you'll be playing Chinese chess, maybe not like a master, but better than the average man in the street.*

How do you play?

Chinese chess is played on a board that looks like this:

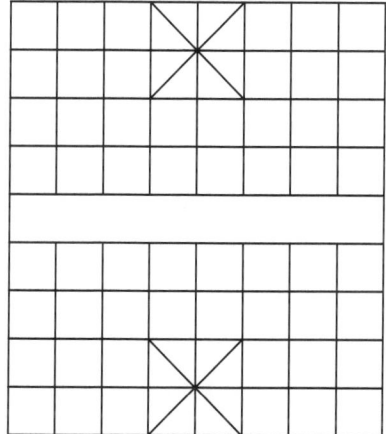

So, mostly like a chess board, but with all the squares the same colour, with an extra blank row in the middle of the board, and with Xs at each end.

The main difference between this and western chess is that the pieces are placed on the intersections at the corners of squares, not in the squares themselves. So in fact, the board has nine columns and ten rows – you'll see more clearly how it works when we put the pieces on the board.

Are the pieces like chess pieces?

Not really. The pieces are circular discs with a Chinese character written on them, to show which piece is which. They are generally written in black for one player and red for the other, and they look like this:

---

* The only mammals that lay eggs are the duck-billed platypus and echidna, although the echidna has a pouch like a kangaroo and keeps the egg in it until it hatches, so there's not much difference between them and marsupials. Platypuses and echidnas also have no nipples, but secrete milk through patches of skin, and the young suck it from the fur covering these patches.

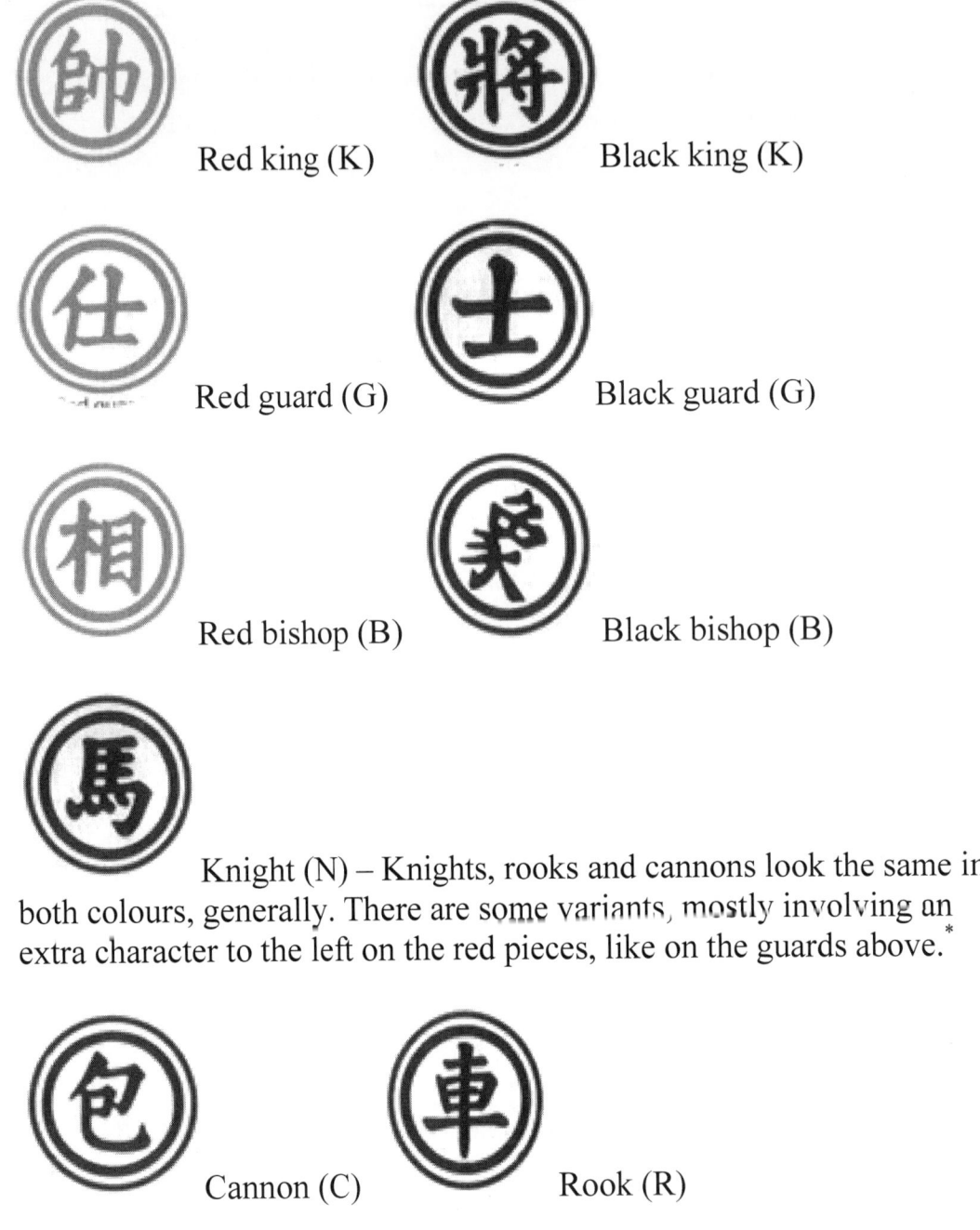

Red king (K)

Black king (K)

Red guard (G)

Black guard (G)

Red bishop (B)

Black bishop (B)

Knight (N) – Knights, rooks and cannons look the same in both colours, generally. There are some variants, mostly involving an extra character to the left on the red pieces, like on the guards above.*

Cannon (C)

Rook (R)

Red pawn (P)

Black pawn (P)

---

* Mr T's real name is Laurence Tureaud.

How do I learn what the characters mean?

It's not as difficult as you might think. The characters evolved from pictures of what they represent – the knight is a horse, with the little legs down at the bottom (sometimes you'll just see them drawn as a wiggly line rather than four distinct marks, but it's still easily recognisable. The cannon, with a bit of imagination, looks like a cannon. The rook looks like a sword, or maybe a castle, depending how you look at it (it's a chariot, in the original Chinese, but that's rather hard to see).*

However, for the rest of the chapter, I'm going to use the names and letters described above. It's a lot easier that way.

How do the pieces move?

Mostly, the pieces move like their chess equivalents, with some differences, as follows:

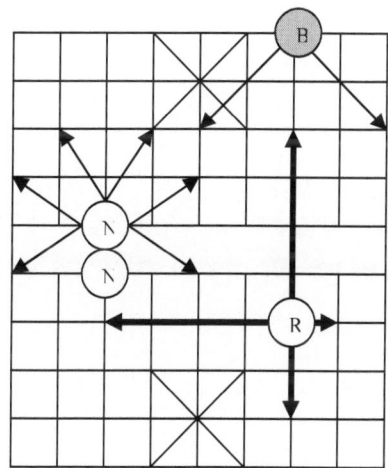 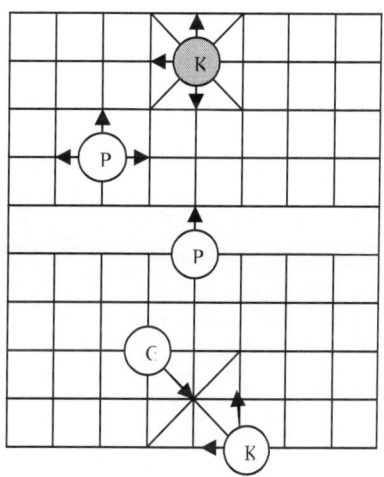

Rooks move exactly like rooks in chess – up, down or across the board, as many ranks or files as you choose, until they bump into another piece. All pieces capture in the same way as chess, by landing on a space occupied by an opponent's piece and removing it from the board.

Knights move almost like their chess counterparts – one space forward or sideways and then one diagonally in the same direction. However, they don't jump, unlike chess knights, which is why it's important to remember that they move one square horizontally or vertically first. A

---

* Famous (nearly) last words: "They couldn't hit an elephant at this distance!" General John Sedgwick, at the Battle of Spotsylvania, 1864. Some sources say he was shot dead by an enemy sniper half way through 'distance', but most reliable witness reports say he managed another sentence before his ironic demise, so his very last words were the much less funny "All right, my man, go to your place."

knight with a piece on the space next to it cannot move in that direction. In the diagram above, the knight can move to six different spaces, but can't go backwards because of the knight in the space behind it.

Bishops in Chinese chess are very limited in their movement. They can only move exactly two squares at a time, diagonally. They are also not allowed to cross the 'river' – the blank row in the middle of the board – meaning that they're stuck in their own half of the board, and can only ever move to one of eight spaces.

Guards are even more limited. They can move only one square diagonally, and they can't leave the 'castle' – the three-by-three box marked with an X on the board. They move along the diagonal lines of the X, and so can only ever move to one of five spaces.

Kings also can't leave the castle, and they can only move horizontally or vertically, one square at a time. They can't move diagonally, unlike chess kings. This gives them a total of nine spaces they can occupy. As in western chess, the aim of the game is to checkmate the king, and kings can't move into check. There's one other rule unique to Chinese chess – kings are not allowed to face each other on the same file without a piece in between them. So in the diagram above, the king at the top of the board can't move to the right, because it would be facing the other king. The king at the bottom can move to the left, because there would be a pawn in between the two kings.

Pawns move one square forward, like chess pawns, until they cross the river. Once they're on the other side of the river, they can move one square either forwards or sideways. This is the only promotion pawns get – unlike chess pawns, if they get to the far end of the board, they're stuck there and can only move sideways from then on.[*]

And what about those cannons?

Well, those are the most interesting piece in the game, at least to people who are used to western chess. They're also the piece that will give you the most advantage over a fellow beginner if you know how to use them properly, so pay attention.

---

[*] More famous nearly last words: "Nobody shot me." Gangster Frank Gusenberg, dying of 22 bullet wounds after the St Valentine's Day Massacre. He actually survived another three hours, and possibly uttered some more, unrecorded, last words following his unhelpful response to the police detective who found him.

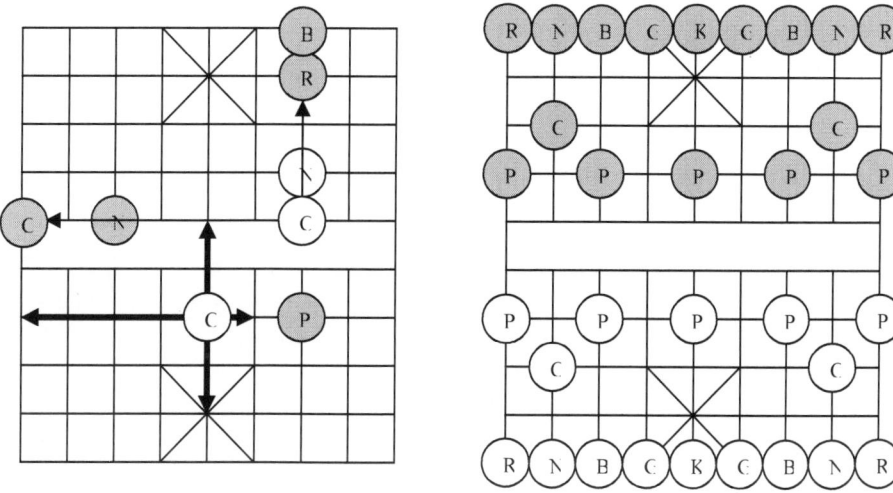

Except when it's capturing, the cannon moves exactly like a rook – horizontally or vertically, as many spaces as it likes. When it's capturing, however, it has to jump over exactly one other piece of either colour. So, in the diagram above, the white cannon on the far bank of the river can capture the black cannon by jumping over the black knight, or the black rook by jumping over the white knight. But it can't take the black bishop, because there are two pieces between that and the cannon. And neither of the cannons can do anything about the black pawn, because there isn't a piece in between them.*

So, what else do I need to know?

The other diagram above shows the starting position. It's pretty much the same as chess, except for there just being five pawns, all starting on the fourth rank, and those two cannons starting on the third. Because pawns only move one square at a time, even on their first move, this brings them together more quickly.

And because pawns capture straight ahead instead of diagonally, and the only diagonally-moving pieces are limited in their range, pawn structure isn't nearly as important in Chinese chess. What is more important is getting the offensive pieces – the rooks, knights and cannons – into good positions as quickly as possible.

A normal opening is to move one of the cannons onto the centre file, where it can threaten the king all the way through the game. Another is to bring the knights forward and towards the centre immediately, and move the pawns in front of them forward so that the knights can advance and the rooks can be developed. The best way to keep the king safe from

---

* Tipp-Ex correction fluid was invented by Bette Nesmith, the mother of Mike Nesmith from the Monkees.

sneaky checkmates is to bring a guard and a bishop in front of it. The two guards can easily defend each other, as can the two bishops.*

How can I win?

The best way to beat a fellow beginner is to be aware of how easy it is to checkmate with the cannons, even with a lot of pieces on the board. Take a look at the following positions:

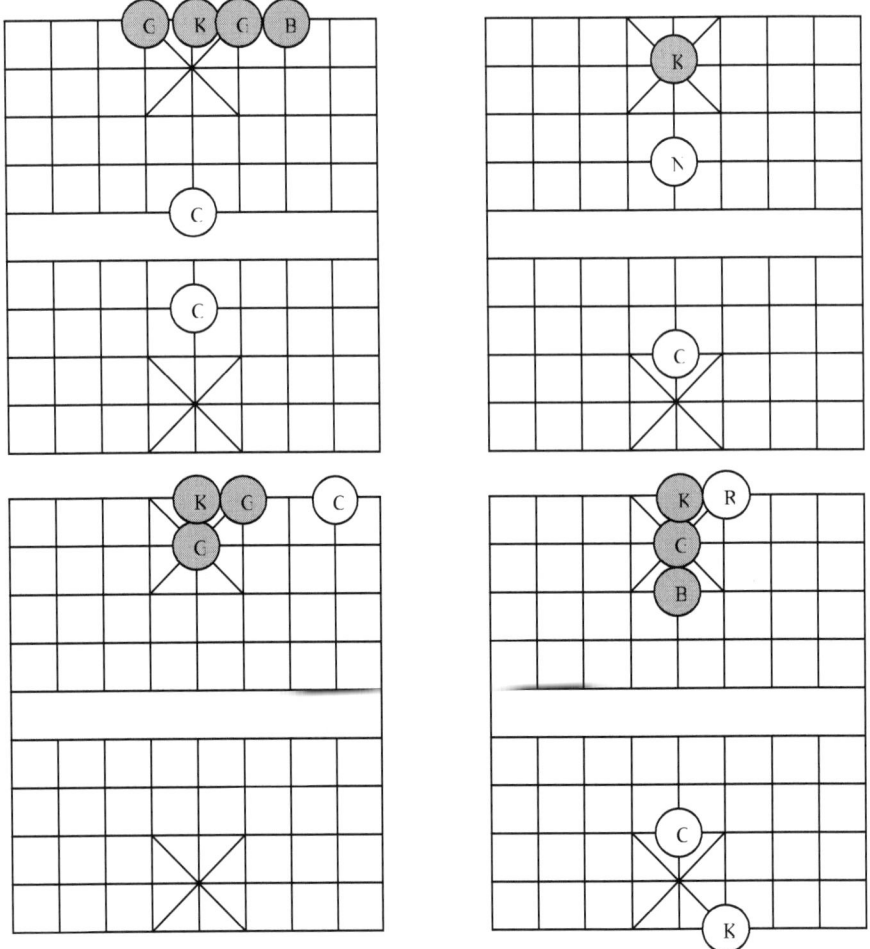

And see how annoying those cannons can be if you didn't see them coming! Now have fun with these games, and you need never play chess again!

---

* The people who created the Monkees planned to follow up their success with a wild-west-themed similar musical TV show and group, called the Kowboys. Frank Welker, the voice of Freddy in Scooby-Doo, was to play the funny Kowboy, Clem. A pilot episode was made, but the series was never commissioned.

How To Calculate Square Roots

I already know how to calculate square roots. You press the button on the calculator that says √.

And if the batteries run out on your calculator? What are you going to do then?

Well, to be honest, I don't really ever need to calculate square roots in the course of an average day.

Fair enough, but this book isn't about teaching you to do anything useful. The point to this is, calculating square roots without a calculator is a lost art. In days of yore, schoolchildren were taught how to do it, but ever since electronic calculators came along, it's disappeared from the maths books. So anyone who can demonstrate how to do this relatively simple thing is going to seem just as impressive as someone who can do complicated quantum physics! Maybe even more so, since you can explain it in ways that ordinary people can understand![*]

Okay, I'm convinced. By the way, what's a square root?

I like to think that this book caters even to the people who really didn't pay attention at school. So, a square root is the number that, multiplied by itself, gives the number you want to find the square root of. The square root of 9 is 3, because 3 times 3 is nine. Okay?

Okay. So what's the square root of 637?

There are actually a lot of different methods out there. Ancient Babylonians, Egyptians, Greeks, Romans all had their own approaches to it. Most of them are based on the principle of taking a guess at the root,

---

[*] Andorra, the tiny country in between Spain and France, declared war on Germany in 1914. This was something of a token gesture, since the Andorran army then consisted of eleven men with no weapons, and there was no fighting, but there was also no peace treaty at the end of the first world war – they were missed off the Versailles treaty. This wasn't noticed until September 25, 1939, by which time the second world war had started. Although you would think he would have had other things on his plate at the time, a German official cheerfully agreed to sign a peace treaty ending the first world war with Andorra. So, technically, the two world wars were actually going on at the same time for twenty-four days.

dividing the number by the guess, taking the average of that result and the first guess, and starting again.

So, for example, we might guess that the square root of 637 is 25 (since a quick mental calculation can tell us that 25 squared is 625). Dividing 637 by 25 gives us 25.48. The average of 25 and 25.48 is 25.24

Dividing 637 by 25.24 gives us approximately 25.2377. The average of the two is 25.23885... and we can keep going like that, but if you check with a calculator, you're already more or less correct to five decimal places.

But the problem with this method is that it involves a lot of long division before you can get to a point where you're sure you've got the answer as accurate as you want it. There is, however, a simpler pen-and-paper method that just takes a bit of multiplication and subtraction, and this one is your best bet for impressing people on the spur of the moment, as well as the one that a lot of unfortunate schoolchildren used to learn!

So why tell me the other one?

I just thought you might be interested. Hey, if it's good enough for Isaac Newton, it's good enough for me.*

Just tell me the good method. I want to go out and impress people.

It's quite simple. Split the number up into pairs, working backwards (or from the decimal point, if you're calculating the root of a non-whole number). Write it down like this:

$$\sqrt{6\ 37}$$

For the first number or pair of numbers, find the closest number matching or below the square root – in this case 2, if the first pair had been 47 it would be 6, and so on. This is the first digit of the answer, naturally:

$$\frac{2}{\sqrt{6\ 37}}$$

---

* While we're talking about Isaac Newton, did you know that as well as discovering gravity and an unimpressive method of calculating square roots, he invented the catflap? Now that's clever.

Just like a division sum at school, put the square of the answer number underneath the first digits, and take it away:

```
       2
    ─────────────
  √ 6  37
    4
    ─
    2
```

Then bring down the next pair of digits:

```
       2
    ─────────────
  √ 6  37
    4
    ─
    2  37
```

And – and here is where we move into unfamiliar territory, so pay attention…

I am paying attention! Get on with it!

Beside this new figure, write down DOUBLE the number you have in your answer so far, with a blank space after it:

```
            2
         ─────────────
       √ 6  37
         4
         ─
  4_     2  37
```

Now we need to find a number to put in the blank, so that if we multiply the completed number by the number we used to fill the blank, we come as close as possible to our bottom line in the sum without going above it.*

So for example, we know we need a number that starts with a 4, that when multiplied by its last digit is as close as possible to 237. 41 x 1 is 41, 42 x 2 is 84, 43 x 3 is 129, 44 x 4 is 176, 45 x 5 is 225, 46 x 6 is 276. Get it? So we need a 5. And the figure that fills the blank space is the next digit of our answer:

---

* Certain famous people in history are known exclusively by their surnames. Clever people could name-drop the full names of people like Grigory Rasputin, Michel de Nostradame (Nostradamus) or the Reverend Wilbert Awdry, if they come up in conversation.

```
              2   5
           ─────────────
          √ 6  37
              4
              ─
              2  37
45 x 5 =      2  25
              ─────
```

Yes, it's confusing, but it's straightforward when you get used to it. Primary school children used to know how to do this.*

Now we repeat the process over and over to get as many decimal places as we want. Bring down the next pair of digits – which, you will remember from school, when you run out of digits in the original number is the first of an infinite string of zeroes after the decimal point – and again put double the answer so far, with a blank space after it, down at the bottom:

```
              2   5 .
           ─────────────────────────
          √ 6  37 . 00  00  00  00
              4
              ─
              2  37
45 x 5 =      2  25
              ─────
             12   00
50_
```

And again, find the right number to fill in the blank. Here it's a 2, because 502 x 2 is 1004, and 503 x 3 is 1509:

```
              2   5 . 2
           ─────────────────────────
          √ 6  37 . 00  00  00  00
              4
              ─
              2  37
45 x 5 =      2  25
              ─────
             12   00
502 x 2 =    10   04
             ─────
              1   96
```

And then carry down the next pair of digits, double the answer so far (ignoring the decimal point) and start again. The multiplication gets harder the further you go, as the answer gets bigger. But you're only ever

---

* Other famous people are known exclusively by their first names – for example, Rembrandt van Rijn, Dante Alighieri and Galileo Galilei.

multiplying by one digit, you can do that in your head, right? And working out a square root to three or four decimal places is as far as you'll ever really need to go:*

```
                    2  5 . 2   3   8   8
                 √ 6 37 . 00  00  00  00
                    4
                    ‾
                    2 37
 45 x 5 =           2 25
                    ‾‾‾‾
                      12 00
 502 x 2 =            10 04
                      ‾‾‾‾‾
                       1 96 00
 5043 x 3 =            1 51 29
                       ‾‾‾‾‾‾‾
                         44 71 00
 50468 x 8 =             40 37 44
                         ‾‾‾‾‾‾‾‾
                          4 33 56 00
 504768 x 8 =             4 03 81 44
```

Wow, we're back at 25.2388 again!

Yes, and without even touching a calculator! Well, unless you used one for those multiplications instead of working them out by hand. Just so we're sure we know what we're doing, here's another sum to work out – this time, we want to know the square root of 89,510,521:

```
                    9  4  6  1
                 √ 89 51 05 21
                   81
                   ‾‾
                    8 51
 184 x 4 =          7 36
                    ‾‾‾‾
                    1 15 05
 1886 x 6 =         1 13 16
                    ‾‾‾‾‾‾‾
                       1 89 21
 18921 x 1 =           1 89 21
                       ‾‾‾‾‾‾‾
                             0
```

---

* The correct plural of 'octopus' is 'octopuses', not 'octopi'. Latin words ending in 'us' end in 'i' in the plural, but 'octopus' comes from the Greek ('octo' meaning 'eight' and 'pous' meaning 'legs'). Some people say this means we should use the Greek plural form 'octopodes', but these people are just being silly. Likewise, the plural of 'hippopotamus' is 'hippopotamuses' (Greek ''ippos' meaning 'horse' and 'potamios' meaning 'river' – why the Greeks thought a hippo looked like a river horse is something that not even clever people know.)

And what do you know? This one works out exactly!*

Is this how computers work out square roots?

No, computers use logarithms. Unfortunate schoolchildren in the olden days were also taught how to use big thick books of log tables to work out things like this. And also slide rules, fascinating devices that only the truly clever people with too much time on their hands know how to use these days. But I won't inflict a chapter on 'How To Use A Slide Rule' on you, readers. One archaic mathematical method is enough for any book.

But I really want to know how to do it now!

Well, maybe in the sequel...

---

* The most boring F A Cup tournament in the long history of the competition was in 1912. After a 0-0 draw after extra time at Crystal Palace on April 20th, the final went to a replay at Bramall Lane the following Wednesday, where Barnsley finally beat West Bromwich Albion 1-0, again after extra time. As if this wasn't dull enough, both semi-finals had also been 0-0 draws, going to replays that were won 1-0. You have to feel sorry for the spectators.

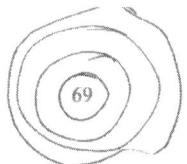

How To Be Creative

Hey, who's been doodling on my book?

That was me, to illustrate lesson one of How To Be Creative – doodle more! Drawing silly pictures and writing the first thing that comes into your head is a good way to unlock your creative impulses and break down your inhibitions, you see.*

What does that have to do with being clever?

Because knowing how to do memory tricks and recite useless trivia can only take you so far. A vital part of being considered a clever person is being able to do something creative on the spur of the moment. And people who doodle are more accustomed to spilling out what's in their head.

I still don't get it.

Sorry. All truly clever people are creative people. And vice versa. Anybody who can dream up a truly funny joke that nobody's ever told before is guaranteed to get a big laugh and an admiring reputation. All those jokes that get told whenever people gather together? Somebody, somewhere, was the first person to think them up, and that person could be you too.

Likewise, anybody who can write a story that people want to read is always going to be regarded as some kind of genius. Anyone who can use their imagination to look at a situation in a way that nobody else has considered is always going to be a success. And developing a vivid imagination plays a big part in the memory techniques that fill three chapters of this book, too.

Okay, I'm convinced. So, how do I become creative?

---

* The longest chapter in the Bible is Psalm 119, which has 176 verses (all about the many good points of the Law of the LORD). The shortest chapter is Psalm 117, which has only two verses (telling everyone to praise the LORD because He is loving and faithful).

It's all about practice. Everybody has an imagination, it's just that some people use theirs a lot, and others don't use theirs at all. Which brings us back to the doodles that are all over this chapter. Consider them a starting point that you can use when you practice your own doodling. Use the margins of the rest of this book, there's plenty of blank space and I don't mind at all. Draw spider webs, pretty patterns, funny animals, dancing octopus-shaped filing cabinets if that's what comes into your head! Embrace your creative side! You'll find it gets easier every time you do it, and your imagination gets wilder. And this is a *good* thing!*

In fact, if I come around to your house and demand to see your copy of this book, I will be very disappointed if the margins of every page aren't filled with scribbles, funny comments on what I've said and drawings of dancing filing octopus-shaped filing cabinets!

You're coming round to my house?

Yes. Make sure you've got biscuits in. Not the ones with chocolate chips, the ones with raisins.

So, how else can I become creative?

Try writing a stream-of-consciousness story. Sit down and write the first thing that comes into your head, and don't try to think about it at all. Keep writing for as long as you can, and once again you'll find it gets easier and more imaginative every time you do it. And, as a side-effect, you might find that your everyday conversation becomes more entertaining and witty, and your lateral thinking ability is enhanced. If you're accustomed to giving free reign to your imagination, you'll be able to think outside the box more successfully in everyday life, because your brain will have got out of the habit of automatically rejecting ideas that seem too strange and unconventional!

Give me an example of stream-of-consciousness writing, please.

I was walking through the woods one day when I noticed a dancing octopus-shaped filing cabinet, juggling rabbits and moving rhythmically to the music created by an oboe which had escaped from the orchestra and returned to the wild. A number of other rabbits, hiding in the bushes to avoid being juggled, could be observed placing bets on which of their

---

* The Koran was dictated in its entirety by Mohammed (peace be upon him), who was illiterate, to various friends, over the course of twenty-three years from 610 to 632.

relatives the filing cabinet would drop first. The rabbit bookie, which was smoking a cigar and wearing an expensive waistcoat, seemed to be doing very good business, which made me worry that the introduction of dancing octopus-shaped filing cabinets to Britain's woodlands, far from making the world a happier place as was the government's intention, had in fact led to a breakdown in moral behaviour among the previously innocent woodland creatures. I also noticed that a blackbird was robbing a bank nearby and stealing all the acorns, while a pygmy shrew was drinking strong alcoholic beverages from a paper bag, although it's possible that these unacceptable activities were not directly related to the filing cabinet's performance. Nonetheless, I shall be writing a fierce letter to the government minister in charge of dancing octopus-shaped filing cabinet woodland distribution.*

You're weird.

Weird and clever. And proud of it.

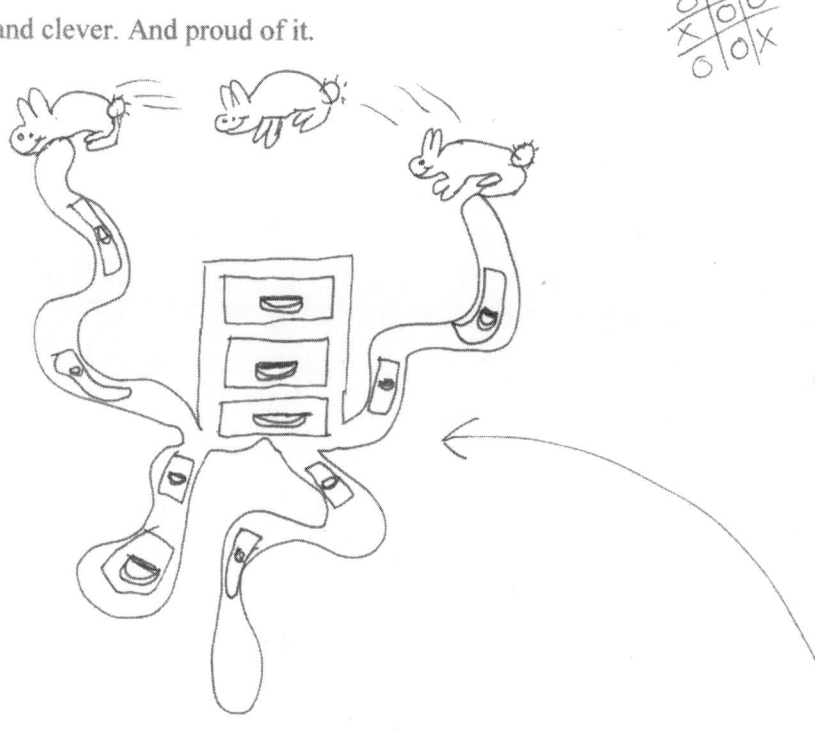

---

* In mammals, gender is determined by X and Y chromosomes – females have two X chromosomes, males have one X and one Y. Some reptiles, birds and insects, however, have W and Z chromosomes – females are WZ while males are ZZ.

I wonder what would happen if you made an animal with YZ chromosomes? Probably this —

How To Win The World Memory Championship

That's not really a party trick.

That's why this is the last chapter. You can ignore it unless you want to know some advanced memory techniques that you might want to use in memory competitions.

So if I learn this I could end up being the World Memory Champion?

Probably not, actually. The thing about memory techniques is that everybody's brain works in a slightly different way. The great memory champions of the past have become great because they've invented their own variations on the basic techniques, that work particularly well for them. So this is really just a guide to the system that I myself use, that I would suggest potential world champions use as just an inspiration for dreaming up their own way of memorising very long numbers.[*]

Okay, so go ahead. I'll just keep quiet.

Good, you were starting to annoy me. This is an expansion of the system detailed in the earlier chapters of this book, on how to memorise cards and numbers. Again using images of objects or people, but this time each object is made from a combination of two playing cards, or three decimal digits, or ten binary digits. The name of the object starts with a one-syllable sound made up of a consonant, a vowel and another consonant. For playing cards, these sounds are made as follows.

The first consonant is given by the combination of suits, like this:

club/club - k
club/diamond - t
club/heart - n
club/spade - m
diamond/club - r
diamond/diamond - d
diamond/heart - l
diamond/spade - g/j

---

[*] Dr Samuel Johnson is known as the man who wrote the first English dictionary, but in fact there had been lots of dictionaries written before his, he just wrote a rather better one which became the British standard. The first English dictionary was Robert Cawdrey's Table Alphabeticall, published in 1604.

heart/club – f/th
heart/diamond - b
heart/heart - h
heart/spade - p
spade/club - sk/sn/sm
spade/diamond - st/sp
spade/heart - sh/sl/sw
spade/spade – s

The vowel comes from the number/rank of the first card, like this:[*]

A = 'a' as in 'cat'
2 = 'e' as in 'pet'
3 = 'i' as in 'kitten'
4 = 'o' as in 'tom'
5 = 'u' as in 'puss'
6 = 'A' as in 'hay'
7 = 'E' as in 'bee'
8 = 'I' as in 'high'
9 = 'O' as in 'low'
10 = 'oo' as in 'you'
J = 'ow' as in 'cow'
Q = 'or' as in 'door'
K = 'ar' as in 'car'

And the final consonant comes from the number of the second card, like this:

A = t
2 = n
3 = m
4 = r
5 = l
6 = g
7 = k
8 = f/th
9 = b
10 = s
J = j/sh/ch
Q = p

---

[*] Neither Cawdrey nor Johnson included any words beginning with X in their dictionaries. Xylophones did exist back then, but they hadn't reached Britain and the word hadn't yet been invented. Nor had X-rays, of course.

K = d

So, for example, Ace of hearts + 2 of clubs gives f (heart/club) + a (Ace) + n (2) = 'fan'. If the 2 of clubs came first it would be n (club/heart) + e (2) + t (Ace) = 'net'.

That gives me 2704 different images. For numbers, I use the same list of images, but only use 1000 of them for decimal and 1024 for binary. It works like this:[*]

First consonant (first digit)

0 = s
1 = t
2 = n
3 = m
4 = r
5 = l
6 = gj
7 = k
8 = f/th
9 = b

Vowel (second digit)

0 = 'oo'
1 = 'a'
2 = 'e'
3 = 'i'
4 = 'o'
5 = 'u'
6 = 'A'
7 = 'E'
8 = 'I'
9 = 'O'

Second consonant (third digit)

0 = s
1 = t

---

[*] X-rays are called Röntgen rays in Germany, after Wilhelm Röntgen, the scientist who didn't discover or invent x-rays, but was the first one to notice that they could be used to photograph bones.

2 = n
3 = m
4 = r
5 = l
6 = g
7 = k
8 = f/th
9 = b

And for binary, it's:[*]

First consonant (first four digits)

0000 = s
0001 = t
0010 = n
0011 = m
0100 = r
0101 = l
0110 = g/j
0111 = k
1000 = f
1001 = b
1010 = p
1011 = d
1100 = h
1101 = sk/sn/sm
1110 = st/sp
1111 = sh/sl/sw

Vowel (next three digits)

000 = 'oo'
001 = 'a'
010 = 'e'
011 = 'i'
100 = 'o'
101 = 'u'
110 = 'A'
111 = 'E'

---

[*] There are 206 bones in a normal adult's body, but some lucky people have more than that – babies are born with somewhere between 300 and 350 bones (it varies), which gradually fuse together over the course of childhood.

Second consonant (final three digits)

000 = s
001 = t
010 = n
011 = m
100 = r
101 = l
110 = g
111 = k

I won't list all 2704 of my images here. While you might possibly benefit from using this system to create your own images, the ones that I use myself almost certainly wouldn't resonate with you. Use your imagination, don't be afraid to bend the rules or make up some silly words for those combinations where you can't find a word to fit the pattern.*

So now I can become world memory champion?

Well, you can certainly give it a try. Good luck!

The End

The end? Am I clever now?

You will be, once you've read our final bit of trivia.†

---

* Adult humans have 32 teeth. Adult dogs have 42, and cats have 30. Humans, cats and dogs all have baby teeth which fall out and are replaced by permanent ones – humans have 20 baby teeth, dogs have 28 and cats have 26. So if you want to make money from the tooth fairy, be a dog or a cat.
† People who are born with a rare genetic condition called anodontia have no teeth at all.

Printed in Great Britain
by Amazon.co.uk, Ltd.,
Marston Gate.